DEDICATION

To family and friends who mean so much to me.

REP

To Garry, Carly, and Amanda
for their many hours of adaptability and support.

CJD

TABLE OF CONTENTS

PREFACE

Story Making: Using Predictable Literature to Develop Communication was written because we have love and respect for children's literature that stems from our work with children who have special needs. As we explored literature, we found a wealth of books available for children to enjoy. In our service delivery model, we have focused on meaningful teaching instead of the "drill-and-skill" method to motivate the population we serve. A firm belief in the benefits of whole language learning has led us to lend even more credence to using printed literature with children.

We hope that *Story Making* will allow those of you who work with children to spend more time accomplishing child-centered goals and less time searching for information. *Story Making* will assist you in planning collaboratively with classroom educators, parents, and caregivers. *Story Making* objectives are cross-referenced to typical curricular themes and communication and thinking goals. Using *Story Making* in a classroom setting ensures that all children, including those with special needs, will benefit from using literature to develop concepts and literacy.

We would like to thank the following people:

Our editors, Kelley Schmidt, Linda Schreiber, and Nancy McKinley, for their exceptional assistance guiding us through our first writing venture, sharing numerous ideas and suggestions, in addition to becoming new friends.

Amanda DeBoer for drawing the first-draft illustrations for our book.

Our students, their educators, and their parents, who enthusiastically used our stories and made us realize their worth.

The authors of trade books who provided the stimuli for our book.

Garry DeBoer and Jim Jones, who thoughtfully reviewed our ideas.

Our reviewers, Ann Gorton, Christina Horde, Jaclyn Neckrich, Sue Prussing, and Peg Reichardt, for field-testing our ideas with children and for sharing their suggestions.

 **INTRODUCTION**

Overview

Story Making: Using Predictable Literature to Develop Communication provides a series of activities to foster communication in children from preschool through grade three who are developing literacy and language. *Story Making* uses the predictable, repetitive phrases from children's favorite literature to generate child-authored books. In these predictable stories, a phrase or sentence is repeated throughout the story, with slight wording changes as the story progresses. The child-authored books can be taken home to encourage further language learning. Forty-four story patterns are provided with suggestions for additional activities. The activities are designed to encourage pre-reading and literacy skills and to meet a child's individualized education program (IEP) goals related to communication, including phonology, semantics, syntax, thinking skills, and written language. Activities are also cross-referenced to mesh with specific curricular themes. Reproducible materials, including story pattern pages, illustrations, parent or caregiver resources and response forms, and forms for monitoring progress are provided for the educator's convenience.

Story Making incorporates whole language philosophy into every lesson and encourages collaboration among professionals and parents and caregivers. The flexible, open-ended activities can be used with a range of language levels and can be adapted for individuals, small groups, and classrooms. Children will author books of their own to share with significant people in their lives, allowing communication to continue at home. *Story Making* really gives children something to talk about!

Goals

The goals of *Story Making* cover a range of literacy and communication skills. These goals include:

1. Exposing children to early literacy experiences in reading, writing, listening, and speaking through the use of quality literature written for children.

2. Developing cognitive and metalinguistic abilities at age-appropriate levels.

3. Providing parents and caregivers with activities that link home-to-school learning.

4. Adhering to whole language principles (i.e., oral and written communication are an integrated process).

5. Encouraging collaborative teaching among educators, and between educators and parents and caregivers, with the outcome being improvement of the child's communication.

Target Population

Story Making is appropriate to use with a variety of children, including those with language disorders and learning disabilities, those learning English as a second language (ESL), and those in general education programs. *Story Making* meets the needs of children in individual and group intervention settings, as well as those involved in collaborative lessons in the classroom. Depending upon children's needs and goals, as well as classroom goals, the books can easily be adapted for use within each of these settings.

The popular trade books (referred to as "model stories") that are the basis for *Story Making* appeal to a wide age range of children. Lessons associated with each model story are flexible enough to use with both preschool children and those in primary grades (kindergarten through grade three). Preschool children will require more guidance when using *Story Making*, while third graders may be more independent and more creative with their work.

Story Making Format

The *Story Making* patterns in this resource build upon concepts and themes found in well-known, easily accessible children's literature. More than 40 lessons and story patterns are included for use with each of the 34 well-known model stories. Each lesson contains possible goals, the overall lesson theme, and suggestions for additional activities.

Initially, educators choose one of the well-known pieces of children's literature (see Table 2, page 17). Educators then read to the children slowly but expressively using phrasing, pauses, and melodic rise and fall of their voices to make the text more meaningful. During this reading time, children remain active participants by repeating the pattern phrase of the specific book, guessing at missing information, and commenting about the story. Following the reading of the story, the teacher helps the children make their own books using the pattern pages supplied in *Story Making*. Books can be made by individual children, by small groups, or in a classroom setting by a large group, depending on the goals to be met.

Educators focus on the specific goals of each child. Children who are working independently can create their own books using the illustrations supplied in *Story Making* to complete the pattern phrase or by creating their own illustrations. Those children who are working in a group setting have the opportunity to work cooperatively while developing metalinguistic skills through discussion about their book. In the classroom setting, children also learn from one another by working together to create a single book. For small and large groups, the created book can be duplicated for the entire class. The books can be taken home for further reinforcement of the intended goals.

Special Features

Educators need organized, goal-related materials at their fingertips. *Story Making* provides suggested goals in the areas of phonology, semantics, syntax, thinking skills, written language, and literacy. These goals are provided in list form on pages 27–29 and are also suggested within each story profile, with the exceptions of written language and literacy goals, which should be embedded within all *Story Making* activities and are not explicitly stated within each story profile. All suggested goals are general. Educators are invited to use these goals but also to write measurable objectives individualized for each child's needs.

Story Making also provides cross-references to aid in choosing a predictable literature resource. Each *Story Making* pattern book has been cross-referenced to the general goals for phonology, semantics, syntax, and thinking skills. In addition, *Story Making* pattern books are cross-referenced to thematic units related to curriculum. The themes can relate to children's classroom and real-life experiences and build on their knowledge of these experiences. The cross-referenced tables, beginning on page 31, are provided for convenience when considering the needs of children.

Forms are also provided to facilitate monitoring of a child's goals or for tracking group lessons. The Monitoring Progress form (see Appendix A) allows educators to monitor the development of specific communication skills for individual children. Educators may use the Lesson Tracking form (see Appendix B) to document and track lessons for both small and large groups. The educator can write either the names of groups or the names of individual children onto this form. After completing a *Story Making* pattern book, the form is dated to document which books have been completed with various groups or individual children. This creates a quick reference guide for planning future lessons.

Story Making also includes a Parent Letter (see Appendix C), a Parent Feedback form (see Appendix D), and an informational handout regarding literacy called *Helpful Hints* (see Appendix E). These forms facilitate the home-to-school link and help educators get feedback regarding the child's communication behaviors at home.

BACKGROUND

Literacy Acquisition

The primary task of children entering school is to make the transition from oral to literate language. Reading, writing, listening, and speaking are all part of communication, and therefore, literacy activities. Researchers refer to the wealth of knowledge many preschool children gain about print before they actually learn to read as *emerging literacy* (van Kleeck, 1990). Before "formal" schooling, children learn something about reading every time they are required to interact meaningfully with print. Children's attention can be directed to print through informal experiences such as reading a sign or a postcard. The need for guidance and support by a literate person has been documented in an array of studies looking at the impact of early literacy experiences on children's acquisition of various aspects of knowledge about print (van Kleeck, 1990). "The objectives of the early stages [of literacy] are to expose students to a literate style of language and to structure opportunities that require specific use of language and facilitate reporting of experiences" (Westby, 1991, p. 350). Literacy skills begin developing at a very early age (i.e., 1½ to 2 years), with skills continuing to build upon one another.

The use of children's literature for class reading and writing instruction helps to create interest in literacy (Creaghead, 1992). Children realize that being read to is a pleasurable activity that can also help them begin to learn about school. One activity that bridges the transition from an emerging reader to a developing reader is shared reading. Materials ideal for shared reading include nursery rhymes, playground rhythms, selected poems, and pattern stories with ritualistic repetition, refrains, and cumulative chants. "Materials for shared reading should be meaningful, memorable, good quality literature which is highly structured, short, energetic, robust, and rhythmically repetitive" (Johnson and Louis, 1990, p. 17). **Story Making** activities that center around shared reading provide opportunities for children to experiment with and develop communication. The use of **Story Making** pattern books in shared reading activities helps each child to make the transition from an emerging reader to a developing reader.

Children need to feel comfortable and "safe" when making errors while they are engaged in literacy activities. "Children need relevant, interesting, and achievable experiences with literacy in warm, tolerant, supportive, and forgiving environments" (Johnson and Louis, 1990, p. 7). Often when demands are placed on children, they "shut down" and do not participate, causing them to have limited practice with literature and linguistic structures. With low-pressure environments, children are allowed to experiment and learn through their "play" with language.

Literacy activities should be relevant to children's experiences and directed at developing all modes of communication. Children learn to deal with meaningful aspects of their lives, and, therefore, if literacy events are meaningful, normal, regular, and reasonably frequent parts of their lives, literacy behavior will develop (Johnson and Louis, 1990). Children are provided with opportunities to develop all modes of communication as they participate in *Story Making* activities. Through the repeated use of both the model stories and the created *Story Making* pattern stories, children are provided the foundation for developing literacy, including reading, writing, listening, and speaking.

Communication Development Through Literature

One of the greatest benefits of using literature as a foundation for learning is the discussion that follows reading activities. As children talk about what they have read, they expand their *metalinguistic skills*—skills used when reflecting on language or using language to talk about language (Haynes and Shulman, 1994). Table 1 (see page 7) reflects the stages of metalinguistic ability identified by Wallach and Miller (1988).

As children become more adept with their communication skills and make the transition from oral to literate language, they begin to use concise syntax, explicit vocabulary, and cohesion based on explicit linguistic markers (Westby, 1991). Children start expanding their basic sentence structure to include more ideas and details, using a greater number and variety of complex grammatical structures. Linguistic abilities emerge as children acquire a better understanding of the story through repeated exposure. This helps them to talk about familiar ideas of daily life situations in increasingly more

Table 1

Stages of Children's Metalinguistic Ability

Stage One (Ages 1½ to 2)

- Distinguishes print from nonprint
- Knows how to interact with books: right side up, page turning from left to right [*sic*]
- Recognizes some printed symbols, e.g., TV character's name, brand names, signs

Stage Two (Ages 2 to 5½ or 6)

- Ascertains word boundaries in spoken sentences
- Ascertains word boundaries in printed sequences
- Engages in word substitution play
- Plays with the sounds of language
- Begins to talk about language parts or about talking (speech acts)
- Corrects own speech/language to help the listener understand the message (spontaneously or in response to listener request)
- Self-monitors own speech and makes changes to more closely approximate the adult model; phonological first; lexical and semantic speech style last
- Believes that a word is an integral part of the object to which it refers (word realism)
- Able to separate words into syllables
- Unable to consider that one word could have two different meanings

Stage Three (Ages 6 to 10)

- Begins to take listener perspective and use language form to match
- Understands verbal humor involving linguistic ambiguity, e.g., riddles
- Able to resolve ambiguity: lexical first, as in homophones; deep structures next, as in ambiguous phrases ("Will you join me in a bowl of soup?"); phonological or morphemic next (Q: "What do you have if you put three ducks in a box?" A: "A box of quackers.")
- Able to understand that words can have two meanings, one literal and the other nonconventional or idiomatic, e.g., adjectives used to describe personality characteristics such as *hard, sweet, bitter*
- Able to segment syllables into phonemes
- Able to resequence language elements, as in pig Latin
- Finds it difficult to appreciate figurative forms other than idioms

From *Language Intervention and Academic Success* (p. 33), by G. Wallach and L. Miller, 1988, Austin, TX: Pro-Ed. © 1988 by Pro-Ed. Reprinted with permission of Pro-Ed and Butterworth-Heinemann.

complex ways (Norris and Damico, 1990). Using *Story Making* offers children the opportunity to develop communication skills and to make the transition from oral to literate language. The model stories read to them provide opportunities for children to hear well-structured language.

Language disorders are thought to be an underlying factor in most literacy learning difficulties (Stanovich, Cunningham, and Freeman, 1984; Kamhi and Catts, 1991; Watson, Layton, Pierce, and Abraham, 1994). Early interactions with print through reading and writing enhance the learning environment for all children, but especially children with language disorders (Watson et al., 1994). The opportunity to experiment with print and to relate print forms with speech acts is crucial to building literacy skills such as reading, writing, listening, and speaking. According to Kamhi and Catts (1991), reading is a language-based skill. Reading problems reflect limitations of language and underlying processing abilities. Therefore, problems in phonology, semantics, syntax, discourse, and narratives are all part of a developmental language impairment that are manifested in successive stages of development from preschool to adult. In determining the causal factors of failure to learn to read, Stanovich et al. (1984) found that in early reading acquisition, multiple factors, not just intelligence, were responsible for predicting reading success in grades one, three, and five. Phonological awareness (i.e., the ability to segment and analyze speech), decoding speed, and listening comprehension (including real-world knowledge, inferential skills, memory strategies, and vocabulary) were major determinants of successful reading comprehension after general intelligence was considered.

Whole Language Philosophy

Whole language philosophy regards communication as a "whole" rather than as segregated parts or components. Listening, speaking, reading, and writing are viewed as a continuum and as interdependent. Oral and written language are viewed as dual functions of communication. Comprehension and production of oral and written language are viewed as one process. Whole language philosophy integrates all elements of communication into the curriculum. Classrooms implementing whole language philosophy are child centered, literature based, talk focused, active, parent involved, fun, and varied (Creaghead, 1992). The goals of *Story Making* adhere to these principles and apply whole language philosophy to language learning.

Some children are not successful in school because they do not meet the language demands of the curriculum (i.e., the content of information in the classroom).

> Whole language programs offer texts which, although they may be conceptually simple, are at least as linguistically complex as the oral language of the children. They encourage children to make language of the text their own through a series of meaningful, open-ended activities. The richness of the language and the open-ended nature of the activities permit individuals to learn those aspects of written language they are "ready" to learn. (Johnson and Louis, 1990, p. 9)

"Whole language specialists contend that the written and oral modes of language have transactional effects on one another, such that oral language can be enhanced through reading and writing and vice versa" (Watson et al., 1994, p. 137).

Story Making provides activities that children at different developmental and linguistic levels can accomplish. Participation is maximized as children are encouraged to read along, predict, and supply a range of appropriate answers, any of which can be correct. Children attend to language content and form, including the sounds of the repetitive phrase, as they listen to and then use this language orally and in writing.

As children's language structures become increasingly more complex, attention can be directed to higher-level communication skills, such as sequencing events, hypothesizing, making inferences, solving problems, identifying cause and effect, making associations, and comparing and contrasting. "Flexibility [in lesson organization] allows the child to develop the ability to reorganize and recombine concepts in thought and language. It allows the child to use the same language in a variety of different contexts" (Norris and Hoffman, 1993, p. 7).

Home Communication

The lives of preschool children are filled with literacy events. However, not all children will have had the same quantity and quality of interaction with print before coming to school. As a result, some children with more limited literacy experience may appear to be "slow" on school entry. They have farther to go than others with richer preschool experiences (Johnson and Louis, 1990). Language development can be promoted through natural activities of daily living such as talking, playing, reading, and writing. Developing literacy begins with doing what those who are literate do already: responding to signs, logos, and labels; sharing books; and scribbling notes. Parents play a vital role at the preschool stage by sharing in these literacy events with their children (Goodman, 1986).

Children begin to make the transition from oral to literate language in the preschool years. Early childhood programs should promote the integration of learning related to themes at school by encouraging the children to bring meaningful contributions from home experiences related to the themes (Wetherby, 1992). This allows children to develop narrative ability and to talk about things familiar to them (e.g., home, play, nature), thereby helping children to make the oral to literate language transition.

Researchers agree that the difference between "home language" and "school language" will frequently result in gaps between ability and performance in class (Simon, 1991). Therefore, children need exposure to literate language and to well-structured oral language to ensure success in school. However, children come to school having different degrees of exposure to literature. Due to their extraordinary circumstances, some preschool children with special needs appear to have less opportunity at home and at school to interact with literacy-related materials as compared to their "normal" peers (Marvin and Mirenda, 1992; Norris and Damico, 1990). Differences in cultural backgrounds can also place a child in an "at-risk" situation in adapting to school language and school scripts (i.e., school routines) (Simon, 1991).

Being read to is one way for beginning readers to have access to literate language (Johnson and Louis, 1990). A parent reading to a child at home will give the child individual reading instruction before entering school. The parent provides what is known as *scaffolding dialogue* by asking the child questions and providing answers when the child cannot answer (Westby, 1991). The interaction time a parent and child spend together reading a book should be a positive experience. This will certainly complement the learning required in school.

Story Making pattern books can be taken home so that generalization occurs in a familiar environment. Bringing home personal copies of pattern books facilitates children's talking about their school experiences using *decontextualized speech* (talking about actions/activities that have occurred in a different situation or context). Use of decontextualized speech is an essential skill that children begin to acquire at approximately age 4 as they gain the ability to discuss events in the past and future. It also allows for subsequent learning. Many children with language disorders have difficulty using decontextualized speech (Wallach and Miller, 1988). Repeated tellings of the same information, story, or procedure to different listeners is a strategy that can help these children bridge the transition from home to school and strengthen the home-to-school link (Norris and Hoffman, 1993). Each *Story Making* pattern book serves as a visual reminder of experiences children have had during the day and facilitates use of decontextualized speech.

Story Making also provides the home-to-school link to literacy that will help bridge gaps in early literacy skills and promote success in school. Children take the newly created books home to show to and talk about with their parents or caregivers. Again, the repeated use of the book fosters a successful communication environment for the child who might not otherwise have the stimulus for communicating.

With *Story Making*, the parents or caregivers have joint responsibility for generalization of skills. Multiple readings of the book at home, in addition to periodically filling out the Parent Feedback form that will be kept in the child's portfolio for evaluation of progress, helps to keep parents and caregivers actively involved in the child's program.

Predictable Stories/Repeated Use

Cumulative or highly repetitive stories are effective in beginning the transition from oral to literate language (Westby, 1991). In predictable books, a phrase or sentence is repeated over and over while one or more of the words are changed. Their familiar content and structure, and the often repetitious, cyclical sequencing of events make these books appealing to children (Goodman, 1986). Patterns are important in making meaning and in learning language. They help children to predict and infer in an authentic context (Montgomery, 1993). The repetition and predictability of the phrase and sentence patterns in predictable literature give children many opportunities to listen to, anticipate, predict, and produce the patterns. These predictable patterns are adapted and used to develop specific communication skills in *Story Making* pattern books.

In addition to the benefits of repetitive patterns in stories, Martinez and Roser (1985) found that children begin to attend to different aspects of a story after repeated readings by a teacher or parent. In their study, the quality and range of the children's responses changed with increasing familiarity with a story. These researchers found that repeated readings lead children to talk more about the story; make more comments rather than answer or ask questions; focus responses on events, details, setting, theme, etc.; and increase processing (make associations between characters and gain greater insight into the story). Thus, repeated readings of the same story allow children to produce more divergent responses. After repeated readings of the well-known model stories, *Story Making* leads to the creation of new stories and the generation of more complex responses.

Reading stories with children fosters vocabulary development, general language development, interest in reading, and success in reading in school (Watson et al., 1994). A story frequently reread reproduces a verbal pattern of words that rapidly becomes predictable. Norris and Hoffman (1993) note, "Written language is useful in facilitating oral language because the print provides a visual, and therefore more contextualized, level of input that the child can use to organize oral language" (p. 223). From this literacy activity, some children will go on to develop a sight vocabulary. Some begin to note sounds and certain spelling patterns (see Table 1, page 7). Some begin to write.

Elizabeth Sulzy (1989) identifies six major categories that exemplify the writing productions of kindergartners. They include (1) writing via drawing; (2) writing via scribbling; (3) letter-like forms; (4) well-learned units; (5) invented spelling; and (6) conventional spelling. All six categories represent information that the children are communicating. *Story Making* provides activities that encourage creativity and imagination through written language as children author their own books. Children write their individual responses, then draw their own representations, if desired.

Routman (1991) suggests using predictable pattern books as a model for writing and reading new stories. Predictable books can be created and illustrated by individuals or by groups of children and then duplicated so each child has a copy. Special educators are now using quality literature, including literature with predictable patterns, to teach reading, with interest level and motivation going up in all grades as a result (Routman, 1991). Once a particular pattern becomes familiar, children can retell and write a parallel version, which is the basis of the ideas in *Story Making*.

Collaboration

As schools begin to adopt an inclusion model, educators will collaborate more and more with each other. *Collaboration* is a fundamental way of working together in a true partnership of sharing problem-solving methods, understanding student learning styles, and developing strategies for student success. As educators work together to enhance functioning in natural learning environments, including the classroom and home settings, new ideas develop, and the benefits to children are obvious. The child with a language-learning disorder may be served best by collaboration between professionals and parents.

In this process, a collaborative team, including parents or caregivers and school staff, plans for the individual needs of the child, assumes cooperative responsibility, and jointly evaluates the child's progress. "Without this collaboration, inclusive education cannot be successful since inclusion is predicated on professionals working together for the purpose of enhancing all the students in the school" (Graden and Bauer, 1992, p. 85).

As educators collaboratively teach, they improve the educational outcomes for all children. Collaboration helps to meet the changing needs of all the children while following the child-centered objectives of the curriculum. ***Story Making*** will meet the needs of educators who are moving forward with collaborative models of teaching. When using this resource in a classroom setting, it can be adapted to each child's needs, since activities are open-ended. During one lesson, children in the same group can focus on a variety of areas such as print versus nonprint skills, writing, and learning language concepts. Thus, the same activity can be used to accomplish a variety of goals, depending on each child's needs.

USING *STORY MAKING*

General Procedures

Story Making presents a process that begins and ends with children immersed in literacy events. Once goals have been determined for each child, the process is initiated by educators and parents, who read popular books with predictable language patterns (i.e., model stories). Children are encouraged to both listen and comment during this reading time. As the predictable language pattern becomes more and more familiar to the children, they are guided through development of their own stories using the *Story Making* patterns provided. The stories created by the children can be shared in class, taken home for further practice, or used for a "launching pad" into related extension activities. The following steps are guidelines for the *Story Making* process:

1. Choose a book based on children's goals using the cross-referenced tables for phonology, syntax, semantics, thinking skills, or curricular themes (see pages 31–43).

2. Read the model story. While reading, have the children begin to infer and say the predictable language pattern of words or phrases. If the children have difficulty, cue them to the predictable pattern used throughout the book (i.e., model the pattern phrase, then prompt the children for responses).

3. As a group, brainstorm ideas for completion of the pattern phrases. (E.g., if the predictable pattern is "I see a ___," children predict what might be on the next page.)

4. Initially, make a book as a class using the children's responses. Direct each child to create one page with his or her response. Collate all pages together to make one book for the classroom.

5. Have each child make a book using the patterns and illustrations supplied with *Story Making*. Children may also illustrate their

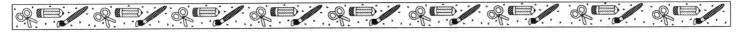

responses or cut pictures from catalogs or magazines. Children should also write their responses on the lines provided (or dictate their responses for an adult to write).

6. Encourage the children to share their individual *Story Making* books by reading them to someone else, such as a classmate.

7. Direct the children to take their *Story Making* pattern books home to read to their parents or caregivers, or to other family members.

8. Send the Parent Letter and the Parent Feedback form (see Appendices C and D) home to help facilitate communication at home as well as to document progress. The handout titled Helpful Hints to Encourage Literacy Skills at Home (see Appendix E) can be sent home at the initiation of the program.

9. Periodically, document individual progress using the Monitoring Progress form provided (see Appendix A).

As stated in these guidelines, choosing a model story is the initial step in using *Story Making*. The choice should be made based on goals targeted for each child.

Table 2, beginning on page 17, provides information about the model stories selected for inclusion in *Story Making*. Each book is listed by title and author, with information about the year of publication and the publishing company included. All of the model stories chosen are popular children's books and can be found in most libraries. (However, the *Story Making* process can be applied to any favorite story that contains a predictable pattern.) Refer to the cross-referenced tables (see pages 31–43) to determine which of the model stories coordinates with a child's goals.

Choosing a Target Story

Thematic Learning

A natural outgrowth of literacy experiences and whole language philosophy is thematic teaching to facilitate language learning. "A thematic unit is an integrated unit only when the topic or theme is meaningful, relevant to the curriculum and students' lives, consistent with whole language principles, and authentic in the interrelationship of the language processes" (Routman, 1991, p. 278). Themes provide a natural connector that helps children begin

Table 2

Well-Known Predictable Literature

Model Story	*Story Making* Pattern Book
Brown Bear, Brown Bear, What Do You See? by Bill Martin, Jr. (1992) New York: Henry Holt	*Snowman, Snowman* *Rainbow, Rainbow*
Is There an Elephant in Your Kitchen? by Ethel and Len Kessler (1987) New York: Simon and Schuster	*Is There a Lion in Your Kitchen?* *Is There a Kangaroo in Your Kitchen?* *Is There a Gorilla in Your Living Room?*
It Looked Like Spilt Milk by Charles Shaw (1947) New York: Harper and Row	*It Looks Like Spilt Milk*
Goodnight Moon by Margaret Wise Brown (1947) New York: Harper and Row	*Good Morning Sun*
Animal Sounds by Aureleuo Battaglia (1981) Racine, WI: Western Publishing	*Animal Sounds*
Whose Toes Are Those? by Joyce Elias and Cathy Strum (1992) Hauppauge, NY: Barron's Education Series	*Whose Toes Are Those?*
King Bidgood's in the Bathtub by Audrey Wood (1985) New York: Harcourt Brace	*Somebody's (or [Child's Name]'s) in the Bathtub*
A Pile of Pigs by Judith Zoss Enderle and Stephanie Gordan Tessler (1993) Honesdale, PA: Boyds Mills Press	*What Is Everyone Doing?*
Mary Wore Her Red Dress and Henry Wore His Green Sneakers by Merle Peek (1985) New York: Houghton Mifflin	*Larry Wore His Red Costume*

(Continued)

Table 2—*Continued*

Model Story	***Story Making* Pattern Book**
Who Says That? by Arnold L. Shapiro (1991) New York: Penguin Books	*Who Says That?*
Going to Sleep on the Farm by Wendy Cheyette Lewison (1992) New York: Dial Books	*Where Do You Go to Sleep?*
The Important Book by Margaret Wise Brown (1947) New York: Harper and Row	*The Important Book*
A House Is a House for Me by Mary Ann Hoberman (1986) New York: Scholastic	*A House Is a House for Me*
What Do You Do with a Kangaroo? by Mercer Mayer (1973) New York: Four Winds Press	*What Do You Do with a Kangaroo?*
Town Mouse and Country Mouse by Janet Stevens (1987) New York: Holiday House	*City Mouse and Country Mouse*
If You Give a Mouse a Cookie by Laura Jaeffe Numeroff (1991) New York: Harper Collins	*If You Give a Bear an Ice Cream Cone*
My Very Own Octopus by Bernard Most (1991) New York: Harcourt Brace	*My Very Own Octopus*
Where Does the Brown Bear Go? by Nicki Weiss (1990) New York: Penguin Books	*Where Does the Brown Bear Go?*
An Egg Is an Egg by Nicki Weiss (1990) New York: Putnam	*A Puppy Is a Puppy*
Guess Where You're Going, Guess What You'll Do by A.F. Bauman (1989) Boston, MA: Houghton Mifflin	*Guess Where You're Going, Guess What You'll Do*

(Continued)

Table 2—*Continued*

Model Story	***Story Making* Pattern Book**
Who Wants One? by Mary Serfozo (1989) New York: Macmillan	*Who Wants One?*
I Wish I Could Fly by Ron Maris (1986) New York: Greenwillow Books	*I Wish I Could Fly*
Who Said Red? by Mary Serfozo (1988) New York: Macmillan	*Who Said Red?*
Have You Seen My Cat? by Eric Carle (1987) Natick, MA: Picture Book Studio	*Have You Seen My Toy?* *Have You Seen My Pet?*
Don't Climb out of ***the Window Tonight*** by Richard McGilvray (1993) New York: Dial Books	*Don't Climb out of the Window* *Tonight*
Sitting in My Box by Dee Lillegard (1989) New York: Dutton	*Sitting in My Tent* *Sitting in My Spaceship*
Little Critter's These Are My Pets by Mercer Mayer (1988) Racine, WI: Western Publishing	*These Are My Pets*
Hide and Snake by Keith Baker (1991) New York: Harcourt, Brace, Jovanovich	*Hide and Snake*
Who Sank the Boat? by Pamela Allen (1982) New York: Coward-McCaan	*Who Sank the Boat?*
Dear Zoo by Rod Campbell (1982) New York: Four Winds Press	*Dear Department Store* *Dear Restaurant*
I Went Walking by Sue Williams (1989) New York: Harcourt, Brace, Jovanovich	*I Went Walking*

(Continued)

Table 2—*Continued*	
Model Story	***Story Making* Pattern Book**
The Dress I'll Wear to the Party by Shirley Neitzel (1992) New York: Greenwillow Books	*This Is What I'll Wear*
This Is the Bear by Sarah Hayes (1986) New York: Lippincott	*This Is the Bunny*
Here Comes a Bus by Harriet Ziefert (1988) New York: Penguin Books	*Here Comes a Bus*
Author-Created Pattern Books by Robin Peura	*The Mouse Book* *The Elephant Book* *How Do You Know?* *Where's the Dinosaur?*

to integrate old and new information. Children who have less flexible language systems do less networking and generalizing of information than their peers, and therefore thematic learning is more critical to these children (Norris and Hoffman, 1993).

Learning materials need to be meaningful so that attention is maintained and optimal learning takes place. Theme teaching allows for organization of information, expansion of preexisting knowledge on a particular topic, reinforcement of target goals, and development of learning strategies. Familiar topics such as people, animals, actions, nature, time, home, and imagination are examples of story themes in *Story Making*. These are themes that are naturally interesting and motivating to young children.

When collaborating with a classroom educator in a whole language program, model stories can be chosen that complement the classroom theme. If educators are not using *Story Making* in a collaborative model, the general education curriculum areas such as science, social studies, guidance, health, math, or other content areas should be explored to determine appropriate themes for children. Children need exposure to and understanding of the world around them through a variety of formats in an integrated curriculum. Selecting a topic or theme that is both developmentally appropriate and compatible with the curriculum as it is presented in the classroom is important to children's needs and interests. A story can be chosen based on themes using the cross-referenced table for themes (see pages 42–43).

Specific Communication Goals

Story Making provides ideas for teaching specific communication goals using literature. The general goal areas included are those most often of concern to the age groups (i.e., preschool through early elementary) this resource addresses. Other areas also may be addressed using the process presented in *Story Making*, and educators are invited to use literature to develop these goals as well.

The goals presented in this resource are general in nature. Measurable objectives will need to be developed based on each child's needs. This section describes the goal areas included in *Story Making*. A general listing of suggested goals begins on page 27, and goals addressed within each *Story Making* pattern book are listed in each story profile.

Phonology Goals

Phonological Process Approach

Story Making supports a phonological process approach to remediation of phonological errors. Analysis of a child's speech is necessary before selecting remediation goals, the management strategy, and the particular story that will be used to develop the phonological pattern. *Story Making* goals are based on Bankson and Bernthal's (1990) phonological process approach to remediation. Bankson and Bernthal (1990) identify 10 phonological processes most frequently used by children: assimilation, fronting, final consonant deletion, weak syllable deletion, stopping, gliding, cluster simplification, depalatalization, deaffrication, and vocalization. Bankson and Bernthal (1990) define these processes as follows:

- Assimilation—replacement of one sound that is the same or similar to a second sound occurring elsewhere in the word.
- Fronting—replacement of a velar sound with one produced further forward in the oral cavity.
- Final consonant deletion—deletion of the final consonant of the word.
- Weak syllable deletion—deletion of an unstressed syllable in a word.

- Stopping—substitution of a stop for a fricative or affricative (occasionally for a liquid).

- Gliding—substitution of a glide for a liquid sound before a vowel.

- Cluster simplification—simplification of a consonant cluster by deletion of one of the consonants, replacement of a cluster with a consonant, replacement of a consonant with another, or omission of the cluster.

- Depalatalization—movement of the place of articulation of a palatal sound from the palate to a position forward in the mouth.

- Deaffrication—replacement of an affricative with a fricative.

- Vocalization—use of a vowel in place of a syllabic or postvocalic liquid.

Once a child's speech is analyzed (using an appropriate phonological process analysis) and goals are developed, a model story can be chosen using the cross-referenced table for phonology (by phonological process) (see pages 32–33). Once chosen, the model story is read so that children can hear the phonological pattern produced appropriately. In most cases, the predictable pattern phrase will model appropriate use of the phonological process identified as a goal in the story profile. Thus, the educator reading the story serves as a model and as a source of auditory bombardment.

As the children create their own books, they should be encouraged to choose responses and illustrations that contain the targeted phonological pattern. Educators can also supply illustrations containing the targeted phonological pattern from other pattern stories. Children can name the illustrations before gluing or drawing them on the pattern pages, followed by saying the pattern phrase, and then saying the whole repetitive verse. Discussion about the illustrations and the pattern book while it is being created is encouraged to provide auditory bombardment of the targeted pattern and to allow opportunities for the child to produce the pattern in conversation. Goals appropriate for remediation of phonological processes can be found on page 27.

Articulation Goals

Traditional phonological remediation using an articulation intervention approach is also possible with *Story Making*. Once the child's speech is assessed, *Story Making* can be used to remediate specific phonemes, including /s, z, l, r, k, g, ð, θ, f, v, t, d, p, b, m, ʃ, and ʧ/. When intervention goals are established, a model story can be chosen using the cross-referenced table for phonology (by phoneme) (see pages 34–35). Once chosen, the model story is read so that children can hear the appropriate production of the targeted phoneme(s). In most cases, the predictable pattern phrase contains the targeted phoneme identified as a goal in the story profile. Thus, the educator reading the story serves as a model and as a source of auditory bombardment.

As the children create their own books, they should be encouraged to choose responses and illustrations that contain the targeted phoneme(s). Children can name the illustrations before gluing or drawing them on the pattern pages, followed by saying the phoneme(s) within the pattern phrase, and then saying the whole repetitive verse. Discussion about the illustrations and the pattern book while it is being created is encouraged to provide auditory bombardment of the targeted phoneme(s) and to allow opportunities for the child to produce the phoneme(s) in conversation. Goals appropriate for remediation of phonemes can be found on page 27.

Goals for Syntactic, Semantic, and Thinking Skills

Story Making addresses specific goals required for successful oral and written communication. The goals are grouped by the language component with which they most often are associated. However, these categories are artificial in a whole language program where all components of communication are integrated. Goals are categorized for ease of use when targeting specific communication skills. Syntactic goals include comprehension and production of various linguistic forms. Semantic goals include concepts of space, time, quality, and quantity. Growth in word knowledge occurs within established themes. Goals for thinking skills include making associations, predicting events, establishing causality, making comparisons, drawing inferences, sequencing, categorizing, and describing functions of objects.

Goals for syntax, semantics, and thinking skills are provided on pages 28–29. When intervention goals are determined, a model story can be chosen using the cross-referenced tables for syntax, semantics, or thinking skills (see pages 36–41). Model stories should then be used to provide appropriate models of the targeted goals, and goals should be reinforced while the children create their own pattern books and read or tell their newly created stories.

Literacy Goals

The underlying intent of *Story Making* is development of literacy in children. Specific goals for literacy will not be found in a cross-referenced table, but rather the expectation is that all *Story Making* activities support

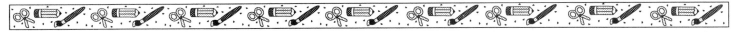

23

the development of literacy. Embedded within all activities is the expectation that children will develop the following literacy skills:

1. Distinguishing print from nonprint.
2. Interacting with books: holding them right side up, turning pages from right to left, interacting with the text from left to right.
3. Recognizing printed symbols.
4. Attending and listening to a story.
5. Describing what is happening in pictures.
6. Identifying the title and author of a book.
7. Identifying characters in a book.
8. Recalling words from a patterned sequence of words.
9. Listening to and identifying rhythmic words.

Written Language Goals

Likewise, written language goals are not to be ignored when using *Story Making*. Written language goals should be embedded within every *Story Making* activity and are not delineated in a cross-referenced table. Educators should be aware that the earliest forms of writing are drawings and scribbles, which are important precursors to the more complex task of forming letters for words. *Story Making* recognizes the following sequence of written language skills:

1. Using a dominant hand for writing.
2. Writing via scribbling.
3. Writing via drawing.
4. Writing letter-like forms.
5. Writing well-learned units.
6. Using invented spelling.
7. Using conventional spelling.
8. Using correct spacing for letters and words.
9. Using correct capitalization and punctuation.
10. Writing basic sentences.
11. Writing complex sentences using cohesion markers.

These skills are listed in a hierarchy. Not all children will achieve the highest levels (i.e., writing basic sentences, writing complex sentences using cohesion markers) using *Story Making*, but educators should be aware of this sequence.

Monitoring Progress

Individual and Group

Story Making provides a Monitoring Progress form in Appendix A to facilitate monitoring of a child's specific communication goals or the goals of a number of children in a small group. The form requires the educator to add goals and measurable objectives based on each child's goals. Objectives can be monitored per *Story Making* lesson. This form can be placed in a portfolio documenting the child's progress.

Home Progress

Story Making also includes resources to help monitor children's communication at home. The following are intended to be sent home with children for parents or caregivers.

A Parent Letter is included in Appendix C. The letter introduces parents and caregivers to the *Story Making* pattern books. It also encourages them to participate in the child's educational program by reading each story with the child and by reinforcing the communication goals at home. The letter reminds parents of the child's specific communication goals. It also gives general suggestions on how to interact with the child when reading the pattern book that is brought home. The date, the child's goal(s), school phone number, and educator's signature need to be added to this letter before sending it home.

Appendix D includes a Parent Feedback form. The form is included to facilitate receiving feedback from parents or caregivers regarding the use of the books at home. The form is designed to take less than five minutes to complete and could be made specific to each book and to each child's individual goals. The returned form can be placed in a portfolio that documents the child's progress at school and home. The date, goals, and educator's signature should be added to this form before sending it home.

A handout titled *Helpful Hints to Encourage Literacy Skills at Home* is included in Appendix E. *Helpful Hints* can be duplicated and sent home to parents or caregivers at the initiation of using *Story Making*. It makes specific recommendations for encouraging communication and literacy at home.

Following this section is a general listing of communication goals for phonology, syntax, semantics, and thinking skills. The goals listed previously for literacy and written language are also included. Educators are reminded to integrate these skills within thematic units.

GOALS

Phonology Goals	
Phonological Processes	**Articulation**
Improve the intelligibility of speech by reducing the use of phonological processes that decrease the intelligibility of speech. 1. Reduce assimilation by producing consonant phonemes in correct sequence. 2. Reduce fronting by producing velar phonemes /k, g/. 3. Reduce final consonant deletion by producing final consonants. 4. Reduce weak syllable deletion by producing unstressed syllables in multisyllabic words. 5. Reduce stopping by producing continuant phonemes /f, v, s, z, ʃ, ð, θ/. 6. Reduce gliding by producing liquids /l, r/. 7. Reduce cluster simplification by producing consonant /s, r, l, n, m/ clusters. 8. Reduce depalatalization by producing palatal phonemes /ʃ, ʧ/. 9. Reduce deaffrication by producing the affricate /ʧ/. 10. Reduce vocalization by producing the syllabic or postvocalic liquids /l, r/, and semivowel /r/.	Improve the intelligibility of speech. 1. Produce the target phoneme in isolation/syllables. 2. Produce the target phoneme in words. 3. Produce the target phoneme in phrases/sentences. 4. Produce the target phoneme during reading. 5. Produce the target phoneme during structured conversation. 6. Produce the target phoneme during spontaneous conversation.

Syntax Goals	Semantics Goals
Comprehend and use linguistic forms:	Comprehend and use basic concepts:

Syntax Goals

Comprehend and use linguistic forms:

1. Forms of negation
2. Verb forms
   - Present tense
   - Present progressive tense
   - Past (regular and irregular) tense
   - Future tense
   - Copula
   - Modal
3. Question forms
   - Yes/no
   - What
   - Whose
   - How
   - Where
   - Who
4. Sentence structures
   - Compound
   - Complex
5. Morphological forms
   - Plurals
   - Articles
   - Possessives
6. Pronouns
7. Descriptions

Semantics Goals

Comprehend and use basic concepts:

1. Spatial concepts
   - Above/below
   - Around
   - Between
   - Beside/next to
   - In/out
   - Inside/outside
   - On
   - Over/under
   - Up/down
   - In front of/in back of/behind
2. Time concepts (morning/night, tonight, until)
3. Quality concepts
   - Size (big/little, larger than/ smaller than)
   - Colors
   - Miscellaneous
4. Quantity concepts (numbers 1–10)

Thinking Skills Goals

1. Make associations.
2. Predict events.
3. Establish causality.
4. Make comparisons.
5. Draw inferences.
6. Sequence events or objects.
7. Categorize objects.
8. Describe functions of objects.

Literacy Goals

1. Distinguish print from nonprint.
2. Interact with books: Hold them right side up, turn pages from right to left, interact with text from left to right.
3. Recognize printed symbols.
4. Attend and listen to a story.
5. Describe what is happening in pictures.
6. Identify the title and author of a book.
7. Identify characters in a book.
8. Recall words from a patterned sequence of words.
9. Listen to and identify rhythmic words.

Written Language Goals

1. Use a dominant hand for writing.
2. Write via scribbling.
3. Write via drawing.
4. Write letter-like forms.
5. Write well-learned units.
6. Use invented spelling.
7. Use conventional spelling.
8. Use correct spacing for letters and words.
9. Use correct capitalization and punctuation.
10. Write basic sentences.
11. Write complex sentences using cohesion markers.

CROSS-REFERENCED TABLES

Cross-referenced tables are provided on the following pages as an information resource for selecting a **Story Making** pattern book. Each pattern book is cross-referenced by goals for phonology, syntax, semantics, thinking skills, and themes. Multiple goals can be targeted by comparing information across tables.

PHONOLOGY (by Phonological Process)

Goal Area	Snowman, Snowman	Rainbow, Rainbow	Is There a Lion in Your Kitchen?	Is There a Kangaroo in Your Kitchen?	Is There a Gorilla in Your Living Room?	It Looks Like Spilt Milk	Good Morning Sun	Animal Sounds	Whose Toes Are Those?	Somebody's (or [Child's Name]'s) in the Bathtub	What Is Everyone Doing?	Larry Wore His Red Costume	Who Says That?	Where Do You Go to Sleep?	The Important Book	A House Is a House for Me	What Do You Do with a Kangaroo?	City Mouse and Country Mouse	If You Give a Bear an Ice Cream Cone	My Very Own Octopus	Where Does the Brown Bear Go?	A Puppy Is a Puppy
Assimilation								●					●									
Fronting			●	●	●	●	●	●						●					●	●	●	●
FCD						●			●	●	●			●	●	●	●		●	●		●
WSD												●			●					●		
Stopping	●	●							●	●			●			●		●	●	●	●	
Gliding	●	●	●	●	●	●						●						●				
CS	●	●				●							●					●		●		
Depalatalization																						
Deaffrication			●	●																		
Vocalization								●		●		●							●			

FCD=Final Consonant Deletion

WSD=Weak Syllable Deletion   CS=Cluster Simplification

Goal Area	Guess Where You're Going, Guess What You'll Do	Who Wants One?	I Wish I Could Fly	Who Said Red?	Have You Seen My Toy?	Have You Seen My Pet?	Don't Climb out of the Window Tonight	Sitting in My Tent	Sitting in My Spaceship	These Are My Pets	Hide and Snake	Who Sank the Boat?	Dear Department Store	Dear Restaurant	I Went Walking	This Is What I'll Wear	This Is the Bunny	Here Comes a Bus	The Mouse Book	The Elephant Book	How Do You Know?	Where's the Dinosaur?
PHONOLOGY (by Phonological Process—*Continued*)																						
Assimilation			•							•	•											
Fronting	•							•	•				•	•				•				
FCD	•				•	•	•	•	•	•	•	•				•					•	
WSD													•			•				•		•
Stopping					•	•				•	•				•	•					•	
Gliding		•	•					•	•	•					•			•	•	•		
CS					•			•	•	•	•	•	•	•					•	•		
Depalatalization			•											•								
Deaffrication																						
Vocalization		•	•										•	•				•	•			•

FCD=Final Consonant Deletion

WSD=Weak Syllable Deletion   CS=Cluster Simplification

PHONOLOGY (by Phoneme)

Goal Area	Snowman, Snowman	Rainbow, Rainbow	Is There a Lion in Your Kitchen?	Is There a Kangaroo in Your Kitchen?	Is There a Gorilla in Your Living Room?	It Looks Like Spilt Milk	Good Morning Sun	Animal Sounds	Whose Toes Are Those?	Somebody's (or [Child's Name]'s) in the Bathtub	What Is Everyone Doing?	Larry Wore His Red Costume	Who Says That?	Where Do You Go to Sleep?	The Important Book	A House Is a House for Me	What Do You Do with a Kangaroo?	City Mouse and Country Mouse	If You Give a Bear an Ice Cream Cone	My Very Own Octopus	Where Does the Brown Bear Go?	A Puppy Is a Puppy
/s/ and /z/	•	•					•	•	•			•	•	•	•	•		•		•	•	•
/l/	•	•	•	•	•	•						•		•				•	•			
/r/ and semivowel /r/		•	•	•	•		•					•										
/k/ and /g/			•	•	•	•	•			•				•				•	•	•	•	•
/ð/ and /θ/									•	•	•		•		•		•				•	
/f/ and /v/																			•	•		
/ʃ/																						
/tʃ/			•	•		•																
/p/, /b/, and /m/						•				•				•				•	•	•		•
/t/ and /d/								•	•	•	•			•	•		•		•	•	•	

PHONOLOGY (by Phoneme—*Continued*)																						
Goal Area \ **Pattern Book Title**	*Guess Where You're Going, Guess What You'll Do*	*Who Wants One?*	*I Wish I Could Fly*	*Who Said Red?*	*Have You Seen My Toy?*	*Have You Seen My Pet?*	*Don't Climb out of the Window Tonight*	*Sitting in My Tent*	*Sitting in My Spaceship*	*These Are My Pets*	*Hide and Snake*	*Who Sank the Boat?*	*Dear Department Store*	*Dear Restaurant*	*I Went Walking*	*This Is What I'll Wear*	*This Is the Bunny*	*Here Comes a Bus*	*The Mouse Book*	*The Elephant Book*	*How Do You Know?*	*Where's the Dinosaur?*
/s/ and /z/					•	•		•	•	•	•	•	•	•	•	•	•	•	•	•	•	•
/l/		•		•				•	•	•					•	•		•	•	•		
/r/ and semivowel /r/			•					•	•				•	•								
/k/ and /g/	•	•	•					•	•		•		•	•				•				
/ð/ and /θ/					•	•	•		•			•	•	•		•	•		•	•	•	•
/f/ and /v/					•	•		•	•		•											
/ʃ/			•																			
/ʧ/																						
/p/, /b/, and /m/					•	•				•		•						•	•	•	•	
/t/ and /d/		•			•	•	•			•		•	•	•							•	•

35

SYNTAX

Goal Area	Snowman, Snowman	Rainbow, Rainbow	Is There a Lion in Your Kitchen?	Is There a Kangaroo in Your Kitchen?	Is There a Gorilla in Your Living Room?	It Looks Like Spilt Milk	Good Morning Sun	Animal Sounds	Whose Toes Are Those?	Somebody's (or [Child's Name]'s) in the Bathtub	What Is Everyone Doing?	Larry Wore His Red Costume	Who Says That?	Where Do You Go to Sleep?	The Important Book	A House Is a House for Me	What Do You Do with a Kangaroo?	City Mouse and Country Mouse	If You Give a Bear an Ice Cream Cone	My Very Own Octopus	Where Does the Brown Bear Go?	A Puppy Is a Puppy
Negation			•	•	•	•				•												
Verb Forms																						
present	•	•				•		•		•			•	•				•				
present progressive											•											
past												•										
future																			•			
copula									•	•					•	•						•
modal																				•		
Question Forms																						
yes/no			•	•	•																	
what	•	•						•			•						•					
whose									•													
how																						
where														•							•	
who									•				•									
Sentence Structures																						
compound										•										•		•
complex					•					•										•	•	•
Morphological Forms																						
plurals									•													
articles	•	•	•	•	•	•		•							•	•	•	•			•	•
possessives									•													
Pronouns	•	•				•			•		•									•		
Descriptions									•			•			•		•			•	•	

SYNTAX—Continued

Goal Area	Guess Where You're Going, Guess What You'll Do	Who Wants One?	I Wish I Could Fly	Who Said Red?	Have You Seen My Toy?	Have You Seen My Pet?	Don't Climb out of the Window Tonight	Sitting in My Tent	Sitting in My Spaceship	These Are My Pets	Hide and Snake	Who Sank the Boat?	Dear Department Store	Dear Restaurant	I Went Walking	This Is What I'll Wear	This Is the Bunny	Here Comes a Bus	The Mouse Book	The Elephant Book	How Do You Know?	Where's the Dinosaur?
Negation		•	•	•	•	•	•					•						•				
Verb Forms																						
present		•					•	•	•	•							•	•			•	
present progressive	•										•										•	
past											•		•	•	•						•	
future	•	•		•												•						
copula					•	•				•	•					•	•	•	•	•		•
modal			•																			
Question Forms																						
yes/no		•		•	•	•						•						•				
what																						
whose																						
how																					•	
where												•										
who															•							
Sentence Structures																						
compound																						
complex			•				•						•	•	•		•	•		•	•	•
Morphological Forms																						
plurals		•																				
articles													•			•	•	•	•	•	•	•
possessives																						
Pronouns		•	•	•	•	•		•	•	•	•		•	•		•	•		•		•	
Descriptions	•										•			•	•							

SEMANTICS

Goal Area / Pattern Book Title	Snowman, Snowman	Rainbow, Rainbow	Is There a Lion in Your Kitchen?	Is There a Kangaroo in Your Kitchen?	Is There a Gorilla in Your Living Room?	It Looks Like Spilt Milk	Good Morning Sun	Animal Sounds	Whose Toes Are Those?	Somebody's (or [Child's Name]'s) in the Bathtub	What Is Everyone Doing?	Larry Wore His Red Costume	Who Says That?	Where Do You Go to Sleep?	The Important Book	A House Is a House for Me	What Do You Do with a Kangaroo?	City Mouse and Country Mouse	If You Give a Bear an Ice Cream Cone	My Very Own Octopus	Where Does the Brown Bear Go?	A Puppy Is a Puppy
Spatial Concepts																						
above/below																					•	
around																					•	
between																					•	
beside/next to																						
in/out			•	•	•					•				•							•	
inside/outside																						
on																					•	
over/under																					•	
up/down																						
in front of/ in back of/ behind																						
Time Concepts																						
morning/night							•															
tonight																						
until																						•
Quality Concepts																						
size (big/little, larger than/ smaller than)																						
colors												•			•							
miscellaneous															•							
Quantity Concepts																						
numbers 1–10																						

Goal Area	Guess Where You're Going, Guess What You'll Do	Who Wants One?	I Wish I Could Fly	Who Said Red?	Have You Seen My Toy?	Have You Seen My Pet?	Don't Climb out of the Window Tonight	Sitting in My Tent	Sitting in My Spaceship	These Are My Pets	Hide and Snake	Who Sank the Boat?	Dear Department Store	Dear Restaurant	I Went Walking	This Is What I'll Wear	This Is the Bunny	Here Comes a Bus	The Mouse Book	The Elephant Book	How Do You Know?	Where's the Dinosaur?
Spatial Concepts																						
above/below											•											
around											•											
between																						•
beside/next to											•											•
in/out							•	•	•		•											
inside/outside																						•
on											•											•
over/under								•	•		•											•
up/down																						•
in front of/ in back of/ behind											•											•
Time Concepts																						
morning/night																						
tonight							•															
until																						
Quality Concepts																						
size (big/little, larger than/ smaller than)								•	•			•	•	•					•	•		
colors				•	•	•																
miscellaneous													•	•								
Quantity Concepts																						
numbers 1–10		•								•												

THINKING SKILLS

Goal Area \ Pattern Book Title	Snowman, Snowman	Rainbow, Rainbow	Is There a Lion in Your Kitchen?	Is There a Kangaroo in Your Kitchen?	Is There a Gorilla in Your Living Room?	It Looks Like Spilt Milk	Good Morning Sun	Animal Sounds	Whose Toes Are Those?	Somebody's (or [Child's Name]'s) in the Bathtub	What Is Everyone Doing?	Larry Wore His Red Costume	Who Says That?	Where Do You Go to Sleep?	The Important Book	A House Is a House for Me	What Do You Do with a Kangaroo?	City Mouse and Country Mouse	If You Give a Bear an Ice Cream Cone	My Very Own Octopus	Where Does the Brown Bear Go?	A Puppy Is a Puppy
Associations	•	•							•		•	•	•	•	•	•		•	•		•	•
Predictions						•							•						•	•	•	•
Causality																			•	•		
Comparisons						•												•				
Inferences									•	•						•	•		•	•		
Sequencing																			•			•
Categorization		•	•	•			•	•	•	•		•										
Functions of Objects																	•		•			

THINKING SKILLS—*Continued*

Goal Area	Guess Where You're Going, Guess What You'll Do	Who Wants One?	I Wish I Could Fly	Who Said Red?	Have You Seen My Toy?	Have You Seen My Pet?	Don't Climb out of the Window Tonight	Sitting in My Tent	Sitting in My Spaceship	These Are My Pets	Hide and Snake	Who Sank the Boat?	Dear Department Store	Dear Restaurant	I Went Walking	This Is What I'll Wear	This Is the Bunny	Here Comes a Bus	The Mouse Book	The Elephant Book	How Do You Know?	Where's the Dinosaur?
Associations				•						•			•	•	•	•	•	•				
Predictions	•						•					•			•		•					
Causality			•				•	•	•				•	•								
Comparisons	•		•					•	•		•	•	•	•					•	•	•	
Inferences	•															•	•	•			•	
Sequencing		•						•	•			•										
Categorization					•	•										•		•				
Functions of Objects			•							•												

Theme \ Pattern Book Title	Snowman, Snowman	Rainbow, Rainbow	Is There a Lion in Your Kitchen?	Is There a Kangaroo in Your Kitchen?	Is There a Gorilla in Your Living Room?	It Looks Like Spilt Milk	Good Morning Sun	Animal Sounds	Whose Toes Are Those?	Somebody's (or [Child's Name]'s) in the Bathtub	What Is Everyone Doing?	Larry Wore His Red Costume	Who Says That?	Where Do You Go to Sleep?	The Important Book	A House Is a House for Me	What Do You Do with a Kangaroo?	City Mouse and Country Mouse	If You Give a Bear an Ice Cream Cone	My Very Own Octopus	Where Does the Brown Bear Go?	A Puppy Is a Puppy
People											•	•										
Jobs													•									
Sports																						
Feelings																						
Animals			•	•	•			•	•		•		•	•			•	•	•	•	•	•
Colors													•		•							
Nature	•	•				•																
Time							•			•				•								•
Home			•	•	•					•						•	•		•		•	
Places to Go												•				•					•	
Actions												•										
Toys																						
Imagination						•											•		•			
Counting																				•		

THEMES—Continued

Theme	Guess Where You're Going, Guess What You'll Do	Who Wants One?	I Wish I Could Fly	Who Said Red?	Have You Seen My Toy?	Have You Seen My Pet?	Don't Climb out of the Window Tonight	Sitting in My Tent	Sitting in My Spaceship	These Are My Pets	Hide and Snake	Who Sank the Boat?	Dear Department Store	Dear Restaurant	I Went Walking	This Is What I'll Wear	This Is the Bunny	Here Comes a Bus	The Mouse Book	The Elephant Book	How Do You Know?	Where's the Dinosaur?
People																						
Jobs															•							
Sports																•						
Feelings																					•	
Animals						•				•	•	•							•	•		•
Colors				•																		
Nature		•					•	•	•		•	•										
Time							•															
Home																						
Places to Go	•							•	•				•	•		•						
Actions			•							•		•				•						•
Toys					•																	
Imagination			•				•	•	•		•							•			•	
Counting		•								•												

STORY MAKING PATTERN BOOKS

Instructions

Each **Story Making** pattern book consists of several pages of master patterns and illustrations to accompany the story. Below are step-by-step directions for creating a **Story Making** pattern book. The directions assume each child will be constructing a pattern book. Adjust these directions when small or large groups are constructing a single book cooperatively.

1. Make one copy of the title page (and second or final pages when appropriate) per book being created. Make several copies containing the pattern phrase that will be used in each book made by the children. Cut all pages apart.

2. Make one copy of the illustration pages for each child, have children make their own illustrations, or have them cut pictures from catalogs and magazines. (Either illustrations or children's art can be used on the pages containing the pattern phrase.)

4. Give each child a title page (and second or final pages when appropriate), several pages with the predictable pattern phrase, and the supplied illustrations (unless children are creating their own art). Provide a scissors, pencil, crayons or markers, and glue or a glue stick for each child.

5. Have the children write their names on the title page.

6. Provide children with the following options for illustrating their **Story Making** pattern book:

   a. Use the illustrations provided. Cut them out, and glue an illustration to complete each response onto each pattern page containing the predictable pattern phrase.

   b. Draw their own responses onto the pattern pages.

   c. Use illustrations cut from catalogs or magazines, or bring pictures from home.

Younger children can cut out and glue the illustrations supplied onto the pattern pages and then dictate their responses for an adult to write in the blanks; older children can write in their own responses on the blank lines and also cut out and glue the illustrations or draw their own illustrations. (If appropriate for younger children, cut out the illustrations ahead of time.) Stories can be as long or short as desired. Allow children to choose their own responses unless a specific illustration is needed to achieve a goal established for the child. Note that children only need to cut around the illustrations to make them fit on the pattern pages; cutting "on the lines" is not necessary.

7. When children have completed their pattern books, staple the pages together or bind them with yarn. Allow children to color their stories as they wish.

8. See suggestions and specific directions in each story profile regarding any unique features of a particular pattern book. A story profile precedes each set of **Story Making** patterns.

9. Allow each child to read or tell his or her created story pattern book. Have children read their stories to each other, to siblings, and to parents or caregivers.

Sample *Story Making* Pattern Book

Figure 1 is an example of a **Story Making** pattern book intended to demonstrate a clear picture of the "final product." Note that the pattern book contains a title page, including the name of the pattern book and space for the child's name as the author. Following the title page, the inside pages contain the printed predictable pattern, with a blank space(s) for the name of the target illustration.

In this example, the child chose the illustrations provided in **Story Making** and glued them onto the pattern page. As shown in the example, the names of the chosen illustrations were written on the blank lines by the child. Children who are not developmentally ready to write should dictate their responses to an adult to write, or they can glue the words found below the **Story Making** illustrations onto the blank line.

Figure 1

STORY MAKING Pattern Book Example

page 2 of the book

Story Making cut-out illustration

Larry wore his green pajamas .
(color) (clothing)

to bed .
(location)

Larry Wore His Red Costume

by Robin Powell

title page

When the books are completed, children read or tell their stories. As children tell their stories or read their created pattern books, they can follow the words printed on the pages. The pattern books may be read in school and then taken home for further reading and learning.

About Story Profiles

Each *Story Making* lesson contains a story profile designed to assist educators in choosing a lesson and expanding literacy activities. The story profiles are a starting point for each educator's creativity; they should not be considered the only options for enhancing learning through *Story Making*.

Story profiles provide information about the model story used in the lesson, including the title, author, publisher information, a brief description of the book's theme, information relevant to special text features, and general reading difficulty level. The predictable language pattern found in the model story is also listed in the story profile. This language pattern is always the basis for the pattern books created by the children. Children will have the opportunity to hear the language in the model story first; they will then hear it and say it again and again as they make and read their own books.

Most *Story Making* lessons include a single pattern book, but several have two or three possible pattern books for children to create. Each story profile includes specific instructions for constructing the particular pattern book.

Story profiles also contain goals for possible target areas in phonology, syntax, semantics, and thinking skills. These goals are suggestions and are not meant to limit the possible uses for *Story Making* pattern books. Educators are encouraged to be creative and flexible as they develop their own goals and objectives using *Story Making*.

Finally, each story profile suggests additional extension activities for each pattern book the children create. Among these suggestions are additional books (often by the same author) to read in school or at home, group activities appropriate for large classrooms or small groups, and creative arts and crafts activities designed to expand learning into other curriculum areas.

The following section contains the story profiles, the *Story Making* pattern books, and illustrations.

Snowman, Snowman
Rainbow, Rainbow

Model Story: ***Brown Bear, Brown Bear, What Do You See?***
by Bill Martin, Jr. (1992)
New York: Henry Holt

Description: This story revolves around various animals looking at each other; finally a fish sees a teacher and some children in a classroom, looking at each other. This 24-page book has one sentence per page and includes very colorful illustrations.

Predictable Pattern: _____, _____, what do you see?
I see _____ looking at me.

Note: The second pages of these pattern books can be found on the bottom halves of pages 52 and 56. For subsequent pages, whatever is the response to the question is the object addressed on the following page.

For example:

(page 2)   Snowman, snowman, what do you see?
I see _a shadow_ looking at me.

(page 3)   _Shadow, shadow_, what do you see?
I see _mittens_ looking at me.

(page 4)   _Mittens_, _mittens_, etc. (Continue until all illustrations are used.)

This story uses the term _snowman_ because it is most familiar to young children. Educators are invited to also include a _snowwoman_ or other _snowpeople_.

Goals:
Phonology: Reduce cluster simplification

Reduce gliding
Reduce stopping
Produce the /s/ phoneme
Produce the /r/ phoneme
Produce the /l/ phoneme

Syntax: Comprehend and use question forms (what)
Comprehend and use morphological forms (articles)
Comprehend and use pronouns
Comprehend and use verb forms (present)

Thinking Skills: Make associations

Theme: Nature

Additional Activities:

1. Additional book to read:
   Polar Bear, Polar Bear, What Do You Hear?
   by Bill Martin, Jr. (1991)
   New York: Henry Holt
   Description: Zoo animals, ranging from a polar bear to a walrus, make their distinctive sounds for each other while children imitate the sounds for the zookeeper.

2. Alter the predictable pattern:

   Polar bear, polar bear,
   what do you *taste?*
   I taste _____.

   Polar bear, polar bear,
   what do you *smell?*
   I smell _____.

   Polar bear, polar bear,
   what do you *feel?*
   I feel _____.

3. Make an interactive language chart by writing on a large piece of tagboard various forms of the pattern phrase. Display the phrases, such as those following, so they are easier for the children to read:

> Snowman, snowman,
> what do you see?
> I see _____
> looking at me.

Direct the children, as a group, to generate responses to complete the phrases.

4. Have the children make snowpeople. First, have each child cut out three circles (small, medium, and large sizes for the head, abdomen, and "legs" of the snowpeople). Next, direct the children to glue the circles on a piece of construction paper. Then let the children make additions with markers and cotton balls to their snowpeople.

5. Make rainbows using colored salt. Divide the children into groups and have them create colored salt by adding food coloring to it. Have each group make one color of the rainbow. Then direct each child to draw an outline of a rainbow on a piece of construction paper, cover each line in the rainbow with glue, and then sprinkle the salt onto the glue. Let the children sprinkle each line of the rainbow with a different color.

6. Take a nature walk with the children. While on the walk (or afterward), say the predictable language pattern using each child's name. Instruct the children to respond with objects they see (or saw) during the walk.

   For example:

   "Matthew, Matthew, what do you see?"
   "I see _____ looking at me."

   The pattern phrase can be altered to include *smell*, *hear*, and *feel*, as described in activity 2.

7. Put objects in a grab bag. Direct each child to reach in and grab an object from the bag. Say the predictable pattern using the child's name (e.g., "Kate, Kate, what do you see?"). Help the child to respond with the name of the object taken from the bag (e.g., "I see _____ looking at me").

Snowman, Snowman

by _____

Snowman, snowman, what do you see?

I see
a shadow
looking
at me.

_____,

_____,

what do you see?

I see _____ **looking at me.**

_____,

_____,

what do you see?

I see _____ **looking at me.**

a tree

a star

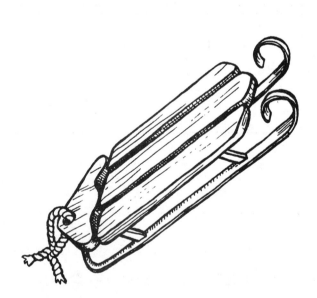

a sled

a reindeer

icicles

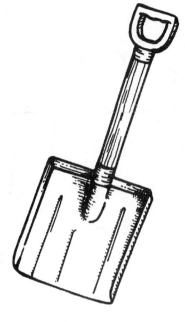

a shovel

boots

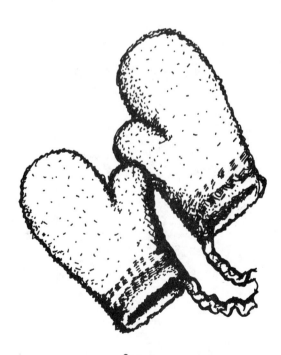

mittens

Rainbow, Rainbow

by _____

Rainbow, rainbow, what do you see?

I see
<u>sunshine</u>
looking
at me.

_____,

_____,

what do you see?

I see _____ **looking at me.**

_____,

_____,

what do you see?

I see _____ **looking at me.**

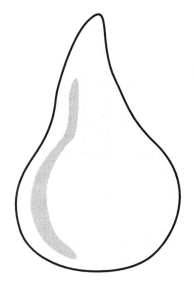

a raindrop

rain

dark clouds

clouds

a tornado

an umbrella

a bird

sunglasses

STORY PROFILES

Is There a Lion in Your Kitchen?
Is There a Kangaroo in Your Kitchen?
Is There a Gorilla in Your Living Room?

Model Story: *Is There an Elephant in Your Kitchen?*
by Ethel and Len Kessler (1987)
New York: Simon and Schuster

Description: Pictures and questions are used to ask whether various items are in your kitchen. The absurdity, "Is there an elephant in your kitchen?" is asked periodically, followed by the response, "Oh! No!" Questions are short (e.g., "Is there a stove?" and "Are there eggs in your refrigerator?"). This 25-page book has large print throughout.

Predictable Patterns:
Is there _____ in your kitchen?
Is there a _____ in your kitchen?
Is there a _____ in your living room?

Note: The pattern pages with the animals in the kitchen/living room (including the phrase "Oh! No!") can be the second pages in these books (following the title page). They can also be placed in the books every three or four pages to continue the pattern. This will add humor and an element of surprise to these *Story Making* books.

Goals:
Phonology: Reduce gliding
Reduce deaffrication
Reduce fronting
Produce the /l/ phoneme
Produce the /r/ and semivowel /r/ phonemes
Produce the /k/ and /g/ phonemes
Produce the /ʧ/ phoneme

Is There a Lion in Your Kitchen?
Is There a Kangaroo in Your Kitchen?
Is There a Gorilla in Your Living Room?

Syntax: Comprehend and use question forms (yes/no)
Comprehend and use forms of negation
Comprehend and use morphological forms (articles)

Semantics: Comprehend and use spatial concepts (in)

Thinking Skills: Categorize objects

Themes: Animals
Home

Additional Activities:

1. Additional book to read:
   Cookie's Week
   by Cindy Ward (1988)
   New York: Putnam
   Description: Cookie the cat gets into a different kind of mischief every day of the week.

2. Discuss and categorize objects that are found in various rooms of a house (e.g., kitchen, living room, dining room, bedroom, bathroom). Write the names of these rooms where everyone can see them. Then categorize various objects that belong in each room. Have the children respond to the pattern phrase, "A _____ belongs in the _____" (e.g., a stove belongs in the kitchen, a bed belongs in the bedroom).

3. Find pictures that contain absurdities. Show the pictures to the children and have them tell about each absurdity, including why it does not make sense (e.g., an elephant lives in the zoo and cannot fit in a house).

4. Categorize objects based on whether they belong inside or outside. Write the categories of *outside* and *inside* where everyone can see them. Then categorize various objects that belong inside a building and outside a building. Let the children name objects, or present them with a predetermined list of objects.

61

Is There a Lion in Your Kitchen?

by _____

Is there a lion in your kitchen?

Oh! No!

Is there _____

in your kitchen?

Is there _____

in your kitchen?

ice cream

cereal

bread

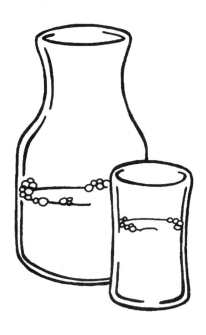

juice

meat

milk

fruit

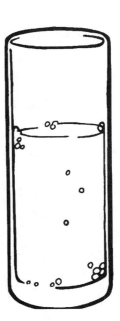

water

Is There a Kangaroo in Your Kitchen?

by _____

Is there a kangaroo in your kitchen?

Oh! No!

Is there a _____
 in your kitchen?

Is there a _____
 in your kitchen?

stove

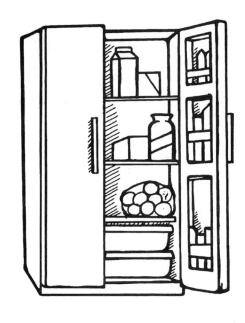

refrigerator

plate

spoon

table

glass

chair

sink

Is There a Gorilla in Your Living Room?

by _____

Is there a gorilla in your living room?

Oh! No!

Is there a _____

in your living room?

Is there a _____

in your living room?

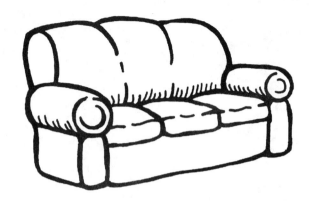

couch

chair

TV

coffee table

lamp

picture

fireplace

rocking chair

 **STORY PROFILE**

It Looks Like Spilt Milk

Model Story: ***It Looked Like Spilt Milk***
by Charles Shaw (1947)
New York: Harper and Row

Description: White illustrations on a blue background show cloud shapes that are similar to a rabbit, a bird, a tree, an ice cream cone, and other objects. There are two sentences per page and very simple sentence structure in this 26-page book.

Predictable Pattern: It looks like a _____, but it's not a _____.

Note: The final page of this book ("It's a cloud in the sky!") is supplied on the bottom half of page 76.

Goals:

Phonology: Reduce fronting
Reduce gliding
Reduce final consonant deletion
Reduce cluster simplification
Produce the /l/ phoneme
Produce the /k/ phoneme

Syntax: Comprehend and use verb forms (present)
Comprehend and use morphological forms (articles)
Comprehend and use pronouns
Comprehend and use complex sentence structures
Comprehend and use forms of negation

Thinking Skills: Predict events
Make comparisons

Themes: Nature
Imagination

**Additional
Activities:**

1. Make cloud formations with paint. Give each child a piece of blue construction paper and put some white paint in the center of the paper. Have the children fold their papers in half. Then open the papers and have the children tell what they think the cloud formations look like.

2. Make cloud formations with various mediums. Use sponge shapes, finger paints, chalk, melted crayons, or cotton balls (pulled apart). Have the children tell what they think the cloud formations look like.

3. Observe the clouds outside. Have each child draw a picture of one of the clouds, and then have other children guess what the cloud looks like.

4. Play a guessing game. Put objects on an overhead projector and have the children guess what each object is. Use objects that children can identify by their outlines (e.g., sponge shapes, puzzle pieces that are whole, keys, pencils, paper clips, rings).

5. Alter the pattern phrase to include the other senses to describe objects.

    For example:
    It sounds like _____.
    It feels like _____.
    It tastes like _____.

It Looks Like Spilt Milk

by _____

It's a cloud in the sky!

It looks like a

_____ ,

but it's not a _____ .

It looks like a

_____ ,

but it's not a _____ .

candle

light bulb

whale

glove

pillow

leaf

lion

lemon

 **STORY PROFILE**

Good Morning Sun

Model Story: *Goodnight Moon*
by Margaret Wise Brown (1947)
New York: Harper and Row

Description: A little rabbit is getting ready for bed. As it gets later and his room grows darker, he bids good night to everything around him. Sentences are short and print is large. The book length is 31 pages.

Predictable Pattern: Good morning _____!

Note: The second page of the pattern book can be found on the bottom half of page 82. Have the children draw a sun on this page.

Goals:

Phonology: Reduce vocalization
Reduce fronting
Produce the /s/ phoneme
Produce the /g/ phoneme
Produce the /m/ phoneme
Produce the semivowel /r/

Semantics: Comprehend and use time concepts (morning/night)

Thinking Skills: Categorize objects

Theme: Time

Additional Activities: 1. Additional book to read:
Runaway Bunny

by Margaret Wise (1977)

New York: Harper Collins

Description: A little rabbit who wants to run away tells his mother how he will escape, but she is always right behind him.

2. Categorize objects by *night* and *day,* such as moon, stars (night) or sun, clouds (day).

3. Discuss daily activities, such as waking up, eating lunch, or putting on school clothes. Sequence these activities by morning, afternoon, and evening activities.

4. Create another pattern book that focuses on the concepts of *before* or *after,* using the pattern phrases:

Before I go to school, I _____.

After I get home from school, I _____.

This is an advanced activity that can be incorporated into curricular goals for learning time concepts.

Good Morning Sun

by _____

Good morning sun!

Good morning _____**!**

Good morning _____**!**

cereal

spoon

washcloth

soap

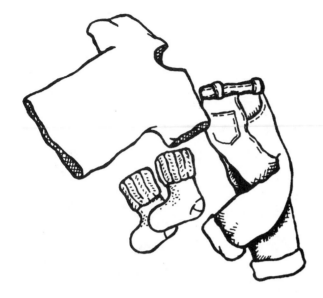

clothes

toothbrush

toothpaste

school bus

 **STORY PROFILE**

Animal Sounds

Model Story: *Animal Sounds*
by Aureleuo Battaglia (1981)
Racine, WI: Western Publishing

Description: In this story, various animals make their sounds. The sentences alternate between question forms and simple sentences. The book has 21 pages with simple, colorful illustrations of the animals.

Predictable
Pattern: What does a _____ say?

Note: The final page of this pattern book can be a self-portrait with something that the child says written below the picture. Use the bottom half of page 88 as the final page.

The following animal sounds can be associated with the animal illustrations provided:

a frog—ribbit! ribbit!
a pig—oink! oink!
a cat—meow! meow!
a dog—arf! arf!
a cow—moo! moo!
a bird—tweet! tweet!
a duck—quack! quack!
a donkey—hee haw! hee haw!

Children should write the sounds in the blanks provided on the pattern page, or they can dictate the sounds to an adult, who writes the sounds in the blank.

Goals:

Phonology: Reduce assimilation
Reduce fronting
Reduce final consonant deletion
Produce the /d/ phoneme
Produce the /s/ and /z/ phonemes

Syntax: Comprehend and use question forms (what)
Comprehend and use verb forms (present)
Comprehend and use morphological forms (articles)

Thinking Skills: Categorize objects

Theme: Animals

Additional Activities:

1. Additional book to read:
   Is Your Mama a Llama?
   by Debra Guarino (1989)
   New York: Scholastic
   Description: A young llama asks his friends if their mamas are llamas and finds out in rhythm that their mothers are other types of animals.

   Use the pattern phrase: Is your mama a _____?

2. Categorize animal names by whether they are baby animals or adult animals. Write the categories of *baby animals* and *adult animals* where everyone can see them. Have children name animals and write each name in the appropriate category. Offer names of animals and have children decide in which category the animals belong.

3. Categorize animals by whether they live on a farm, in the zoo, or in a pet store. Write the categories of *farm*, *zoo*, and *pet store* where everyone can see them. Direct children to name various animals that belong in each category. Add animals to those suggested by the children.

Animal Sounds

by _____

What do
you say?

_____

What does a

_____

say?

_____
(animal sound)

What does a

_____

say?

_____
(animal sound)

frog

pig

cat

dog

cow

bird

duck

donkey

STORY PROFILE

Whose Toes Are Those?

Model Story: *Whose Toes Are Those?*
by Joyce Elias and Cathy Strum (1992)
Hauppauge, NY: Barron's Education Series

Description: Pictures of the toes of various animals are accompanied by poems that describe but do not name the animals. On pages that follow, the animal is named and revealed. Sentences are long in the rhyming description of the animal. This 45-page book has large print (i.e., the animal name, when it is revealed, is in gigantic print).

Predictable
Pattern: Whose toes are those? Those are _____.

Note: The pattern pages for this story require children to write or dictate a description of the feet they see in an illustration. (E.g., for a duck's toes, a child might write, "The animal's toes are orange. There are two webbed feet.") Children should select an illustration, describe it on one page, then glue the picture on the following page that has the predictable pattern. The last page of the book is on the bottom half of page 94. Children should draw a picture of their own toes on this page; they do not need to write anything.

Goals:
Phonology: Reduce vocalization
Reduce final consonant deletion
Reduce stopping
Produce the /z/ phoneme
Produce the /ð/ phoneme
Produce the /t/ phoneme

Syntax: Comprehend and use question forms (whose)
Comprehend and use morphological forms (possessives, plurals)
Comprehend and use verb forms (copula)
Use linguistic forms in descriptions

Thinking Skills: Draw inferences
Categorize objects
Make associations

Theme: Animals

Additional Activities:

1. Additional books to read:

   Guess What?
   by Beau Gardner (1985)
   New York: Lothrup, Lee, and Shepard
   Description: The reader examines an illustration of part of an animal's body and tries to guess the identity of the animal, which is revealed in the complete illustration on the next page.

   Whose Footprint?
   by Masayuki Yabruuchi (1985)
   New York: Philomel Books
   Description: Various animals make different tracks.

2. Make a mural of people's feet. Cut out magazine pictures of people's feet. Paste the pictures on a large sheet of paper. Have the children infer associated characteristics with each set of feet.

3. Make footprints of a variety of animals going different places. Have the children guess which animal left each set of footprints and where the animal might be going.

4. Draw a very large footprint on a large piece of tagboard. Have the children guess how many of their footprints would fit inside. Begin tracing children's footprints inside the large footprint. Have the children count the total number of footprints that are made.

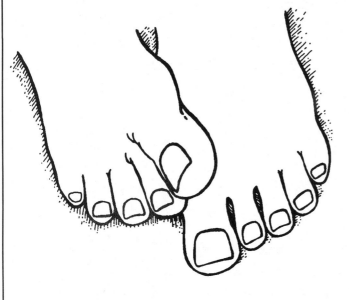

Whose Toes
Are Those?

by _____

Whose toes are those?

Those are my toes!

_____

_____

_____

_____

(description)

Whose toes are those?

Those are _____ .

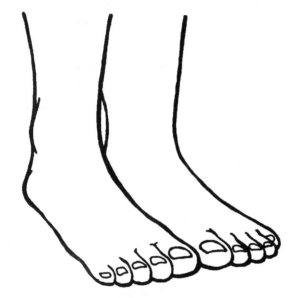

a person's toes

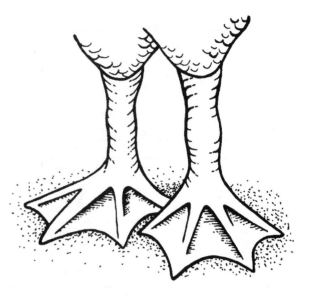

a duck's toes

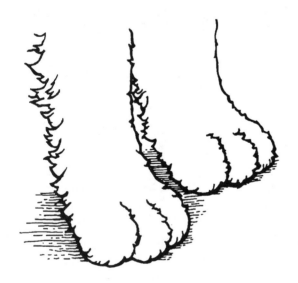

a dog's paws

a bear's paws

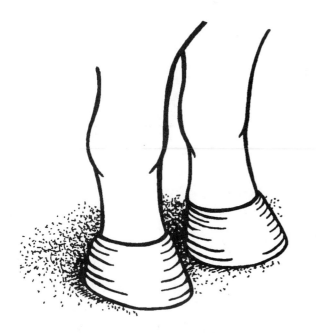

a horse's hooves

an elephant's toes

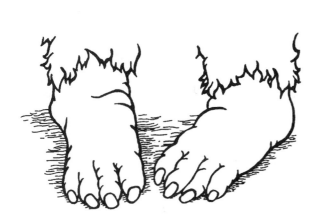

a gorilla's toes

a tiger's paws

97

STORY PROFILE

*Somebody's (or [Child's Name]'s)
in the Bathtub*

Model Story: *King Bidgood's in the Bathtub*
by Audrey Wood (1985)
New York: Harcourt Brace

Description: A fun-loving king refuses to get out of the bathtub to rule his kingdom. The entire court fails to persuade him to leave his tub. The surprise ending comes when a royal page solves the dilemma by pulling the plug! The book length is 32 pages. There are one to three lines per page in large print.

**Predictable
Pattern:** _____'s in the bathtub and won't get out. Oh! Who knows what to do? Give (it/him/her) a _____.

Note: A friend or relative's name, the child's name, or a pet's name can be written on the title page and on appropriate subsequent pages (i.e., containing either it, him, or her).

Goals:
Phonology: Reduce final consonant deletion
Reduce stopping
Produce the /ð/ and /θ/ phonemes
Produce the /b/ phoneme
Produce the /t/ and /d/ phonemes
Produce the /g/ phoneme

Syntax: Comprehend and use question forms (who)
Comprehend and use forms of negation
Comprehend and use complex sentence structures
Comprehend and use compound sentence structures
Comprehend and use verb forms (copula, present)
Comprehend and use pronouns

Semantics: Comprehend and use spatial concepts (in)

Thinking Skills: Categorize objects
Draw inferences

Themes: Home
Time

Additional Activities:

1. Additional book to read:
   The Napping House
   by Audrey Wood (1984)
   New York: Harcourt, Brace, Jovanovich
   Description: In this cumulative tale, a wakeful flea atop a number of sleeping creatures causes a commotion with just one bite.

2. Make an interactive language chart by writing on a large piece of tagboard various forms of the pattern phrase. Display the phrases, such as those following, so they are easy for the children to read:

   ┌─────────────────────────────────┐
   │ _____'s in the bathtub   │
   │ and won't get out.   │
   │ Oh! Who knows what to do?   │
   │ Give him a _____.   │
   └─────────────────────────────────┘

   ┌─────────────────────────────────┐
   │ _____'s in the bathtub   │
   │ and won't get out.   │
   │ Oh! Who knows what to do?   │
   │ Give her a _____.   │
   └─────────────────────────────────┘

   Direct the children, as a group, to generate responses to complete the phrases.

3. Sing "Rub-a-Dub-Dub" or "Rubber Ducky" as a group.

4. Show the video version (which puts the text of the story to music) of ***King Bidgood's in the Bathtub*** (1985) by Random House Video, SRA/McGraw-Hill, Blacklick, OH.

_____'s

in the
Bathtub

by _____

_____'s

in the bathtub and

won't get out. Oh!

Who knows what

to do?

Give it a

_____.

_____'s

in the bathtub and

won't get out. Oh!

Who knows what

to do?

Give him a

_____.

_____'s

in the bathtub and

won't get out. Oh!

Who knows what

to do?

Give her a

_____.

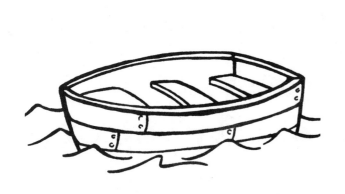

boat

duck

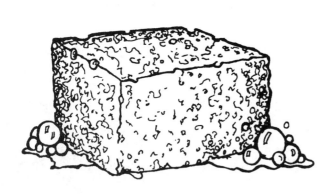

sponge

bucket

squirt gun

bar of soap

bottle of shampoo

washcloth

STORY PROFILE

What Is Everyone Doing?

Model Story: *A Pile of Pigs*
by Judith Zoss Enderle
   and Stephanie Gordan Tessler (1993)
Honesdale, PA: Boyds Mills Press

Description: A group of farmyard pigs forms a pyramid to see what the cows are doing on the other side of the barn. What are the cows doing? Making a pyramid to see what the pigs are doing! Sentences range from three to seven words per page and include quotations, dialogue, and a compound sentence structure. The book is 21 pages in length.

Predictable Pattern: What is the _____ doing?
The _____ is _____.

Note: Either people or animals can be used in this pattern story. The following actions are associated with the pictures provided:

The horse *is galloping.*   The boy *is climbing.*
The elephant *is carrying.*   The girl *is jumping.*
The bear *is licking.*   The mom *is waving.*
The pig *is eating.*   The dad *is driving.*
The dog *is barking.*   The grandma *is smiling.*
The seal *is balancing.*   The grandpa *is sleeping.*
The tiger *is running.*   The baby *is crawling.*
The fish *is swimming.*   The family *is eating.*

Direct children to write (or dictate) these actions in the blank provided.

104

Goals:

Phonology: Reduce weak syllable deletion
Produce the /d/ phoneme
Produce the /ð/ phoneme

Syntax: Comprehend and use question forms (what)
Comprehend and use verb forms (present progressive)
Use linguistic forms in descriptions

Thinking Skills: Make associations

Themes: People
Animals
Actions

Additional Activities:

1. Have children bring magazine pictures of people performing actions to class. Have them describe the actions and then make a collage.

2. Determine several actions for one animal (e.g., a horse can gallop, jump, trot, and run). Write the actions where everyone can see them. Have the children demonstrate the actions and discuss how the actions compare to one another (e.g., galloping is faster than trotting).

3. Compare children's actions to babies' actions, and then compare children's actions to animals' actions.

   Use the pattern phrases:
   Children _____ but babies _____.
   Children _____ but animals _____.

   For example:
   Children walk but babies crawl.
   Children talk but animals make noises.

4. Pantomime actions (as in charades) and have the children guess what the actions are. Ask the question, "What is _____ doing?" Then ask children to respond (e.g., "She is cooking," "He is reading").

What Is Everyone Doing?

by _____

What is the

_____

doing?

The _____ is _____.

What is the

_____

doing?

The _____ **is** _____.

What is the

_____

doing?

The _____ **is** _____.

horse

elephant

bear

pig

dog

seal

tiger

fish

boy

girl

mom

dad

grandma

grandpa

baby

family

STORY PROFILE

Larry Wore His Red Costume

Model Story: *Mary Wore Her Red Dress and Henry Wore His Green Sneakers*
by Merle Peek (1985)
New York: Houghton Mifflin

Description: This story is based on an Australian folksong. A group of animals wear different colored clothing items to a birthday party. Colors mentioned in the book contrast with black and white illustrations in the background. The sentences are highly repetitive, with one to two per page. The length of the book is 20 pages.

Predictable Pattern: Larry wore his _____ to _____.

Note: Children choose one of the illustrations provided with this pattern book and color the illustration in various colors. For example, children might color the jacket red and use *red* in the pattern phrase, "Larry wore his *red jacket* to the *park*." Or color the jeans blue and use *blue* in the pattern phrase, "Larry wore his *blue jeans* to *school*." The color and clothing item are written on the first blank line. Children choose a second illustration representing the location, which is written on the second blank line.

Goals:
Phonology: Reduce vocalization
Reduce gliding
Produce the /l/ phoneme
Produce the /z/ phoneme
Produce the /r/ and semivowel /r/ phonemes

Syntax: Comprehend and use verb forms (past)
Comprehend and use pronouns

Semantics: Comprehend and use quality concepts (color)

Thinking Skills: Make associations
Categorize objects

Themes: Colors
People
Places to go

Additional Activities:

1. Additional book to read:
   Jesse Bear, What Will You Wear?
   by Nancy White Carlstrom (1986)
   New York: Macmillan
   Description: Rhythm, text, and illustrations describe Jesse Bear's activities and clothing changes from morning to bedtime.

2. Make paper dolls. Have the children draw the dolls and cut them out. Suggest that the children draw the dolls' clothing items in a fashion similar to the illustrations provided in the pattern book.

3. Trace the children's bodies on large mural paper and instruct the children to draw clothes on their body outlines. Have them draw clothes related to places they may be going, such as a party, or school. The children can also draw the places in the background.

4. Make a pattern book for one location and include all of the items associated with that place (e.g., balls, sandals, goggles, tubes, and shovels would all be brought to the beach). Use the pattern phrases:

   _____ brought his _____ to the _____.
   _____ brought her _____ to the _____.

5. Make a silly story by mixing and matching the illustrations at random. Discuss why it would be absurd. For example, "Larry wore his pink pajamas to school."

Larry Wore His Red Costume

by _____

Larry wore his _____
(color)   (clothing)

to _____.
(location)

114

Larry wore his _____
(color)   (clothing)

to _____.
(location)

Larry wore his _____
(color)   (clothing)

to _____.
(location)

jacket

bathing suit

dress-up clothes

pajamas

116

the park

the beach

the party

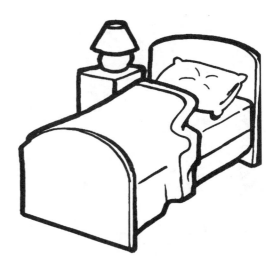

bed

jeans

jogging suit

apron

baseball cap

school

the gym

art class

the game

STORY PROFILE

Who Says That?

Model Story: *Who Says That?*
by Arnold L. Shapiro (1991)
New York: Penguin Books

Description: Animals and the sounds they make are written in two-word sentences. The book includes colorful illustrations of the animals. The phrase, "But girls and boys make different noise!" is repeated every four or five pages.

Predictable Pattern: Who says that?
The _____ says "_____."

Note: Two sets of illustrations are provided for this pattern book: animals and their associated sounds, and people working in various occupations and their associated phrases. The first blank should be completed by filling in the name of a community helper or animal. The second blank should be completed with the phrase related to the occupation or the animal's sound. The pattern on the bottom half of page 122 that says, "But boys and girls make different noises," should be repeated every four or five pages and should also be used as the last page of the book.

Goals:
Phonology: Reduce final consonant deletion
Reduce stopping
Reduce assimilation
Produce the /s/ and /z/ phonemes
Produce the /ð/ phoneme

Syntax: Comprehend and use question forms (who)
Comprehend and use verb forms (present)

Thinking Skills: Make associations
Predict events

Themes: People (jobs)
Animals

Additional Activities:

1. Show pictures of hats associated with a variety of different occupations (e.g., a chef's hat, a baseball cap, a sailor's hat, a police officer's hat). Help the children name the occupation relating to each hat and associated activities performed by people in that occupation.

2. Have the children describe what they want to be when they grow up. Use the pattern phrase:

   When I grow up, I want to be _____.

   Then, make predictions about what each child in the class will be when he or she grows up.

3. Instruct the children to cut out pictures of people from newspapers or magazines and glue them on paper. Help them to write captions appropriate for each person to say in his or her job (e.g., a picture of the president might have a caption saying, "We want peace"; a caption for a flight attendant might say, "Fasten your seatbelt").

Who Says That?

by _____

But boys and girls

make different noises.

Who says that?

The _____ says

" _____ ."

Who says that?

The _____ says

" _____ ."

rooster

sheep

lion

bee

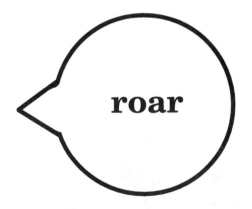

125

monkey

seal

goat

owl

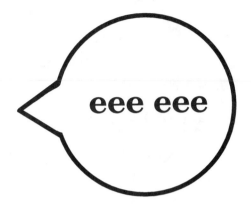

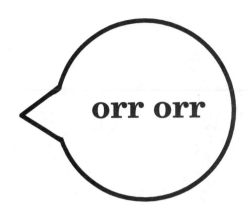

crossing guard

doctor

police officer

barber

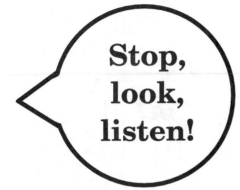

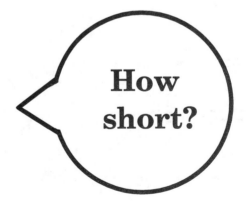

129

firefighter

mechanic

grocery clerk

plumber

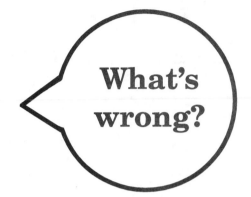

STORY PROFILE

Where Do You Go to Sleep?

Model Story: ***Going to Sleep on the Farm***
by Wendy Cheyette Lewison (1992)
New York: Dial Books

Description: Using a question-and-answer format and rhyme, a little boy asks his dad where farm animals sleep. Simple, soft color illustrations fill each page of this 23-page book and verses are repeated throughout.

Predictable Pattern: Where does a _____ go to sleep? Tell me where a _____ goes to sleep.

A _____ goes to sleep in _____.

Note: Use the pattern found on the bottom half of page 134 as the last page of the book. Children can draw pictures of their own beds on this pattern page.

Goals:
Phonology: Reduce fronting
Reduce cluster simplification
Reduce final consonant deletion
Produce the /z/ phoneme
Produce the /l/ phoneme
Produce the /g/ phoneme
Produce the /d/ and /t/ phonemes
Produce the /m/ phoneme

Syntax: Comprehend and use question forms (where)
Use linguistic forms in descriptions
Comprehend and use morphological forms (articles)
Comprehend and use verb forms (present)

Semantics: Understand and use size concepts (in)

Thinking Skills: Make associations

Themes: Animals
Time

Additional Activities:

1. Additional book to read:
   Good Night Owl
   by Pat Hutchins (1972)
   New York: Macmillan
   Description: Because the noises of other animals keep him from sleeping, Owl watches for a chance to take his revenge.

2. Have each child describe the sequence he or she follows when getting ready for bed. Discuss similarities and differences in the children's bedtime routines.

3. Go to a zoo or a farm. With the children, make a list of animals that are sleeping along with the locations where they are sleeping.

4. Make an absurd or silly story by mixing and matching at random the illustrations provided (e.g., match *cow* with *nest;* match *mouse* with *tree*). Discuss why the combination would be absurd.

5. Create a pattern story using negation. Use the pattern phrase:

   Where does a _____ go to sleep? Tell me where the _____ goes to sleep.

   For the response, use the pattern phrase:

   _____ does not go to sleep in a _____. (E.g., a *horse* does not go to sleep in a *web.*)

   As an option, use the illustrations provided with this pattern book to complete the sentence.

Where Do You Go to Sleep?

by _____

I go to sleep in my bed!

Where does a _____ go to sleep?

Tell me where a _____ goes to sleep.

A _____ goes to sleep in _____.

Where does a _____ go to sleep?

Tell me where a _____ goes to sleep.

A _____ goes to sleep in _____.

bird

cow

dog

bear

a nest

a barn

a doghouse

a cave

137

spider   **mouse**

lion   **dolphin**

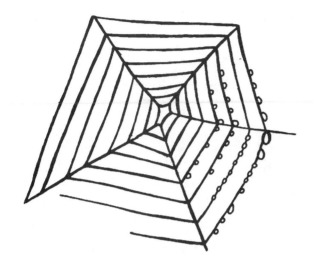

a web

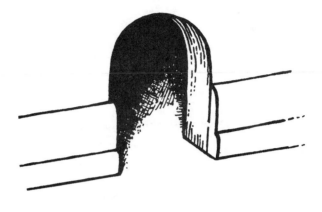

a hole

the jungle

an ocean

 **STORY PROFILE**

The Important Book

Model Story: ***The Important Book***
by Margaret Wise Brown (1947)
New York: Harper and Row

Description: This book discusses basic feature concepts (color, taste, shape, smell) of several common objects and why these features are important. A variety of print styles are used throughout this 19-page book, with three to four sentences per page.

Predictable
Pattern: The important thing about _____ is _____.

Note: This pattern book requires more extensive writing on the part of children and may be more appropriate for older children. The final page of the book can be found on the bottom half of page 143. Children should draw pictures of themselves on this pattern page.

Goals:
Phonology: Reduce final consonant deletion
Reduce weak syllable deletion
Produce the /θ/ and /ð/ phonemes
Produce the /t/ phoneme
Produce the /z/ phoneme

Syntax: Comprehend and use verb forms (copula)
Comprehend and use morphological forms (articles)

Semantics: Quality concepts (color, misc.)

Thinking Skills: Draw inferences
Make associations

Themes: Home
Places to go
Colors

**Additional
Activities:**

1. Brainstorm with the children about who is important in their lives. Make a list of these people where everyone can see it. Write the reasons the children give for why these people are important to them.

2. Have each child bring in a picture of someone important. Pictures can be photographs of family members or friends, or they can be magazine pictures of important people (e.g., the president of the United States, a favorite TV character, etc.). Mount the picture on a bulletin board and have each child describe why the person he or she selected is important.

3. Ask the children to bring in photographs of themselves. Place each photograph in the center of a sheet of paper. Then have each child draw persons who are important to him or her around the photograph and describe why each person is important.

4. Create a chart on a large piece of tagboard. Divide the chart into three columns and label the columns *most important, important,* and a *little important.* Have the children think about the "things" in their lives that are important to them. Encourage them to rank their important things from most important to a little important. Write each child's responses in the appropriate column followed by his or her name. Point out the differences in what each of the children finds important.

5. Using the children's responses of activity 4, direct each child to tell the important features of each "thing." Include concepts of size, shape, color, etc.

6. Write a list of jobs and occupations where everyone can see them. Be sure to include jobs and occupations

familiar to the children (e.g., principal, cook, bus driver, police officer, crossing guard). Encourage the children to generate reasons why these jobs are important.

7. Discuss objects that are important for daily living, such as a telephone, car, stove, etc. Make a list of these objects, then discuss why they are important. For example: a telephone is important because you can talk to friends, your mom and dad, or call 911 in an emergency. A car is important because you need it to ride to school, take a trip, get to the grocery store, etc. Talk about how life would be different if people didn't have important things like telephones or cars.

The Important Book

by _____

The important thing about me

is _____

_____ .

The important thing

about

_____

is

_____

_____.

The important thing

about

_____

is

_____

_____.

parents

**a brother or
a sister**

a teacher

a student

a telephone

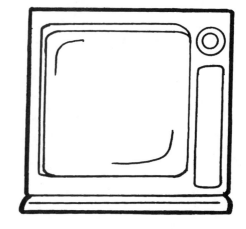

a TV

a kitchen

toys

a pencil

a library

a computer

a school bus

a bed

a pet

a playground

a chalkboard

148

STORY PROFILE

A House Is a House for Me

Model Story: *A House Is a House for Me*
by Mary Ann Hoberman (1978)
New York: Scholastic

Description: This rhyming book describes animals and their homes (such as a bee and a hive). Various kinds of housing for humans are also described. Colorful, detailed illustrations make this book interesting to look at. Sentences range from one to eight words, with sentence structure ranging from simple to complex. This book is 45 pages in length.

Predictable Pattern: _____ is a house for _____.

Note: There are two sets of illustrations available for use with this *Story Making* pattern: animals and their homes, and objects and the places where they belong.

The final page for this story is supplied on the bottom half of page 151. Children can draw their own house on this page, below the phrase "This is the house for me."

Goals:

Phonology: Reduce final consonant deletion
Reduce stopping
Produce the /s/ and /z/ phonemes

Syntax: Comprehend and use morphological forms (articles)
Comprehend and use verb forms (copula)

Thinking Skills: Make associations

Theme: Home

Additional Activities:

1. Additional book to read:

   Need a House? Call Ms. Mouse
   by George Mendoza (1981)
   New York: Grosset and Dunlop

   Description: Henrietta designs and builds unusual houses for animals but admits she likes the simple life. This encourages readers to think about their own likes and dislikes.

2. Visit a zoo or a farm. Observe where each animal lives (e.g., in water, inside a building, in a small cage, in the ground). Make a graph or chart with the children showing where they observed the animals living.

3. Orally present analogies and have the children supply missing information. The following are examples:

   Nest is to bird as house is to _____.

   Web is to spider as water is to _____.

   Cave is to bear as desert is to _____.

   Forest is to fox as tree is to _____.

   Barn is to cow as pond is to _____.

A House Is a House for Me

by _____

This is the house for me.

_____

is a house for _____.

_____

is a house for _____.

A nest

A doghouse

A tree

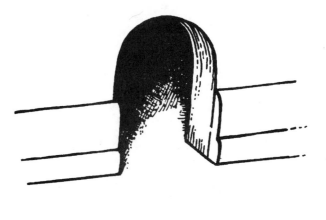

A hole

153

a bird

a dog

an owl

a mouse

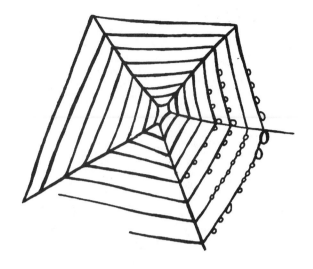

A web

A cave

A jungle

An ocean

a spider   **a bear**

a lion   **a dolphin**

A shoe

A glove

A bowl

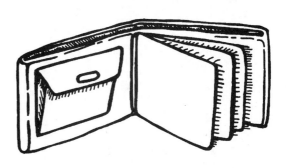

A wallet

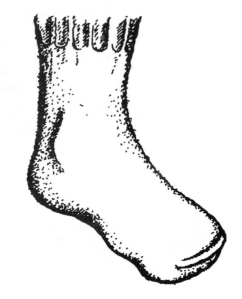

a foot

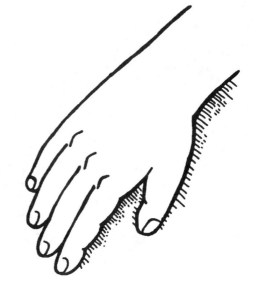

a hand

cereal

money

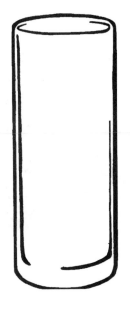

A glass

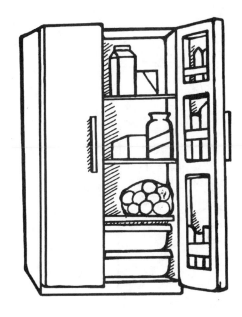

A refrigerator

A library

A bed

milk

food

books

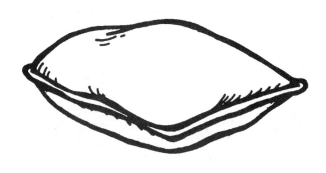

a pillow

STORY PROFILE

What Do You Do with a Kangaroo?

Model Story: ***What Do You Do with a Kangaroo?***
by Mercer Mayer (1973)
New York: Four Winds Press

Description: A variety of animals show up in a little girl's home, requesting that she make them more comfortable. When she tries to make the animals leave, they refuse—so she lets them stay. There are four to five sentences per page, with sentences including dialogue, questions and answers, and compound and complex structure.

Predictable
Pattern: What do you do with _____?

Note: Two sets of illustrations are provided with this ***Story Making*** pattern, allowing children to choose either animals or objects to illustrate their books. Children can use their imaginations to determine what to do with the animals. Answers to the question "What do you do with _____?" can be written in the blanks provided, either by the children or by an adult who writes as each child dictates.

Goals:
Phonology: Reduce final consonant deletion
Produce the /t/ and /d/ phonemes
Produce the /θ/ phoneme

Syntax: Comprehend and use question forms (what)
Use linguistic forms in descriptions
Comprehend and use morphological forms (articles)

Thinking Skills: Draw inferences

Describe functions of objects

Themes: Animals

Imagination

Additional Activities:

1. Additional book to read:

There's a Nightmare in My Closet
by Mercer Mayer (1968)
New York: Dial Books
Description: A little boy solves the problem of what to do with a nightmare in his closet: simply tuck it in bed with you to make it happy.

2. Make up riddles using descriptions of various objects, such as:

I clean your hands.
I'm usually found in the bathroom.
Sometimes I smell good.
What am I? (I am soap.)

I am round.
I am up in the sky.
I shine during the day.
What am I? (I am the sun.)

I have four legs and a tail.
I live in homes.
I bark.
What am I? (I am a dog.)

Help the children to make up their own riddles and share them with the group. Continue until all children have had a turn.

3. Have the children pantomime their responses to questions such as, "What do you do with a book?" (the child pantomimes *reading*), or "What do you do with a car?" (the child pantomimes *driving*).

What Do You Do with a Kangaroo?

by _____

What do you do with

_____?

_____

_____

What do you do with

_____?

What do you do with

_____?

a tiger

a horse

a snake

a fish

a frog

a seal

a dog

a cow

books

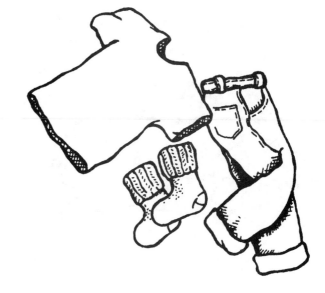

clothes

food

boots

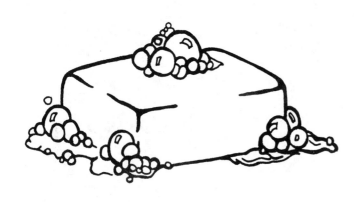

soap

a TV

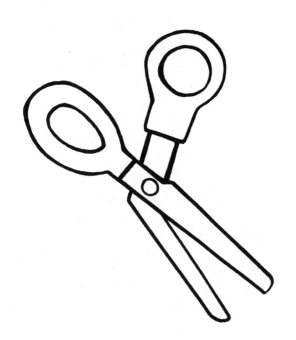

scissors

keys

City Mouse and Country Mouse

Model Story: ***Town Mouse and Country Mouse***
by Janet Stevens (1987)
New York: Holiday House

Description: A town mouse and country mouse exchange visits and discover that each is suited to his own home. This book is 28 pages in length. Simple, short sentences are used in large print.

Predictable Pattern: City mouse likes _____.
Country mouse likes _____.

Note: Alternate the pages in the book to contrast the items that city mouse likes with the items that country mouse likes. The last page of the book can be found on the bottom half of page 171.

Goals:

Phonology: Reduce cluster simplification
Reduce stopping
Reduce gliding
Produce the /m/ phoneme
Produce the /s/ phoneme
Produce the /k/ phoneme
Produce the /l/ phoneme

Syntax: Comprehend and use verb forms (present)

Thinking Skills: Make comparisons
Make associations

Themes: Animals
Home

Additional Activities:

1. Act out the story as a play. Use common objects as props to add interest.

2. Make comparisons between the farm and city. Use the pattern phrase:

   On the farm, you _____, but in the city, you _____. (E.g., on the farm, you walk in the pasture, but in the city, you walk on a sidewalk.)

3. Make an interactive language chart by writing on a large piece of tagboard various forms of the pattern phrase. Arrange the phrases, such as those following, so they are easy for the children to read:

   ┌─────────────────────────────┐
   │ I drove my big _____   │
   │ through the _____   │
   │ and over the _____   │
   │ to get my _____.   │
   └─────────────────────────────┘

   Example: I drove my big _truck_
             through the _field of animals_
             and over the _bridge_
             to get my _overalls_.

   Use illustrations from other **Story Making** patterns, including _Larry Wore His Red Costume_ and _Here Comes a Bus,_ to complete the phrases. Or, direct the children, as a group, to generate responses to complete the phrases.

City Mouse and Country Mouse

by _____

Each mouse likes his own house best.

City mouse likes

_____

_____ .

Country mouse likes

_____

_____ .

a skyscraper

a limousine

the highway

a mansion

a zoo

a restaurant

a swimming pool

a city bridge

a barn

a truck

a dirt road

a cabin

a field of animals

a picnic

a pond

a country bridge

STORY PROFILE

If You Give a Bear an Ice Cream Cone

Model Story: *If You Give a Mouse a Cookie*
by Laura Jaeffe Numeroff (1991)
New York: Harper Collins

Description: Giving a cookie to a mouse begins a sequence of events that becomes funnier as this book goes on. Colorful illustrations and simple sentence structure (one to two sentences per page) make this book very appealing. Predicting what the mouse will do next is an important part of this 28-page story.

Predictable Pattern: If you give a bear _____, he'll want to _____.

Note: The pattern book should be organized as a sequence of events with the initiating event being "giving a bear an ice cream cone" (use the bottom half of page 179). The children should predict what would happen if the bear was given the illustrated objects, then write their responses on the blank line.

For example:
(page 2)   If you give a bear an ice cream cone, he'll want to _eat it_.
(page 3)   If you give a bear a piece of gum, he'll want to _chew it_.

Goals:
Phonology: Reduce final consonant deletion
Reduce stopping
Reduce vocalization
Reduce fronting
Produce the /b/ phoneme

Produce the /g/ phomeme
Produce the /t/ phoneme
Produce the /f/ and /v/ phonemes
Produce the /l/ phoneme

Syntax: Comprehend and use verb forms (future)
Comprehend and use pronouns
Comprehend and use complex sentence structures

Thinking Skills: Draw inferences
Make associations
Predict events
Describe functions of objects
Sequence events
Establish causality

Themes: Animals
Imagination

Additional Activities:

1. Additional book to read:
   If You Give a Moose a Muffin
   by Laura Jaeffe Numeroff (1991)
   New York: Harper Collins
   Description: This is a humorous story emphasizing cause and effect. It begins when a muffin is offered to a moose.

   Make cookies and muffins following a recipe. Let the children eat the cookies or muffins after reading the story. Encourage discussion about the book's theme.

2. Have the children write or dictate a sequence of how they get to school.

3. Use associated word pairs to complete the pattern phrase, such as:

   If you get a present, you will want to _____.
   If you get a dollar, you will want to _____.
   If you get stung by a bee, you will want to _____.
   If you get wet, you will want to _____.

If You Give a Bear an Ice Cream Cone

by _____

If you give a bear
an ice cream cone,
he'll want to

_____

_____.

If you give a bear

_____

_____,

he'll want to

_____

_____.

If you give a bear

_____

_____,

he'll want to

_____

_____.

an ice cream cone

a camera

a piece of gum

music

peanut butter
and jelly

blocks

a guitar

crayons

182

STORY PROFILE

My Very Own Octopus

Model Story: *My Very Own Octopus*
by Bernard Most (1991)
New York: Harcourt Brace

Description: A boy imagines the many advantages of having an octopus for a pet. Counting how many times the octopus
could shake the boy's hand or give him a hug (which
would, of course, be eight) makes this book fun to use
for practice counting. This 28-page book contains two to
three compound or complex sentence structures per
page.

**Predictable
Pattern:** If I had my very own octopus, I would _____.

Note: Use the pattern found on the bottom half of page 185 as
the last page of this book. Each child can draw a picture
of his or her own octopus on this pattern page.

Goals:
Phonology: Reduce fronting
Reduce final consonant deletion
Reduce weak syllable deletion
Reduce stopping
Produce the /m/ phoneme
Produce the /s/ phoneme
Produce the /k/ phoneme
Produce the /f/ and /v/ phoneme
Produce the /d/ phoneme

Syntax: Comprehend and use verb forms (modal)
Comprehend and use complex sentence structures

Comprehend and use compound sentence structures

Use linguistic forms in descriptions

Thinking Skills: Predict events

Draw inferences

Establish causality

Themes: Animals

Counting

Additional Activities:

1. Additional book to read:

   If the Dinosaurs Came Back

   by Bernard Most (1984)

   New York: Harcourt Brace

   Description: This creative story describes the various everyday jobs that dinosaurs could help us with if they came back to life.

   Use the pattern phrase:

   If the dinosaurs came back, I would _____.

2. Make a mural of the ocean. Have the children find or draw pictures of water animals, such as shrimp, fish, octopus, seahorses, whales, and seals. Attach the pictures to the mural on the bulletin board.

3. Draw an octopus with eight enlarged legs and display it where everyone can see it. Write a two-step direction on each leg (e.g., put your name and today's date on your paper, find your name and put it in a pocket, take off your coat and hang it up). Have the children choose a direction, then follow it.

4. Discuss the kinds of activities children can do with their pets, such as sleeping with them, riding in the car with them, and playing outside with them. Go through the activities depicted in the book, ***My Very Own Octopus***, and determine if the activities shared by the boy and the octopus could really happen or if they are only make-believe.

My Very Own Octopus

by _____

And that's what I would do
if I had my very own octopus.

If I had my very own octopus, I would

_____

_____

_____.

If I had my very own octopus, I would

_____

_____

_____.

sing and dance

hop and skip

throw and catch

comb my hair and brush my teeth

187

color and cut

drink and eat

**make my bed and
pick up my toys**

**wash the dishes
and put them away**

STORY PROFILE

Where Does the Brown Bear Go?

Model Story: *Where Does the Brown Bear Go?*
by Nicki Weiss (1990)
New York: Penguin Books

Description: The question asked is, "Where do the animals go at night?" It is followed by the repetitive response, "They are on their way. They are on their way home." The book contains 22 pages with large print.

Predictable
Pattern: Where does _____ go?

Note: The animals pictured in this story are in various locations. Children need to identify locations, such as *between the trees, on the branch, in the cave,* or *under the leaves,* and write these phrases on the blank lines provided on the pattern pages.

For example: Where does the *leopard* go?
between the trees

Add the pattern page, "They are on their way. They are on their way home" every three or four pages. It is on the bottom half of page 191. Have the children draw several animals on this page.

Goals:
Phonology: Reduce fronting
Reduce stopping
Reduce cluster simplification
Produce the /ð/ phoneme
Produce the /z/ phoneme
Produce the /g/ phoneme
Produce the /d/ phoneme

189

Syntax: Comprehend and use question forms (where)
Comprehend and use morphological forms (articles)
Use linguistic structures in descriptions

Semantics: Comprehend and use spatial concepts (between, in, on, above/below, over/under)

Thinking Skills: Make predictions
Make associations

Themes: Animals
Home
Places to go

Additional Activities:

1. Visit a zoo or watch a videotape of animals. Observe where the animals live. Afterward, see how many locations the children can remember from their observations.

2. Provide stuffed animals or have the children each bring a stuffed animal from home. Hide the stuffed animals in the classroom. Direct each child to find one of the animals. When found, ask the child where the animal was hiding. Then have the child describe the stuffed animal (e.g., name where the animal came from and why the child likes the particular animal).

3. Show the children pictures of a variety of different animals from the same species. Compare and contrast the different animals (e.g., how is a kitten different from a lion/how are they alike?).

Where Does the Brown Bear Go?

by _____

They are on their way.
They are on their way home.

Where does

_____

go?

_____

_____

(place)

Where does

_____

go?

_____

_____

(place)

the leopard

the fish

the eagle

the kangaroo

the zebra

the chimpanzee

the hamster

the spider

194

STORY PROFILE

A Puppy Is a Puppy

Model Story: ***An Egg Is an Egg***
by Nicki Weiss (1990)
New York: Putnam

Description: "Nothing stays the same. Everything can change" is the theme of this book about eggs becoming chickens, seeds becoming flowers, and children becoming grown-ups. This 29-page book has large print and one to two sentences per page.

**Predictable
Pattern:** A _____ is a _____ until it grows up and becomes _____.

Note: This pattern book requires children to select two illustrations per page—one illustration of the baby animal and one picture of the associated adult animal. The pattern page with the phrase, "Nothing stays the same. Everything can change," found on the bottom half of page 197, can be inserted periodically throughout the pattern book (similar to the way this phrase is used in the book ***An Egg Is an Egg***).

Goals:
Phonology: Reduce final consonant deletion
Reduce fronting
Produce the /z/ phoneme
Produce the /p/ and /b/ phonemes
Produce the /k/ phoneme

Syntax: Comprehend and use morphological forms (articles)
Comprehend and use verb forms (copula)

Comprehend and use compound sentence structures
Comprehend and use complex sentence structures

Semantics: Time concepts (until)

Thinking Skills: Predict events
Make associations
Sequence events

Themes: Animals
Time

Additional Activities:

1. Additional book to read:
   Are You My Mother?
   by P.D. Eastman (1960)
   New York: Random House
   Description: When a mother bird leaves the nest, her egg hatches and the baby bird goes looking for her.

2. Have the children draw pictures of their family members, arranging them from youngest to oldest. Ask children to name and describe each person.

3. Have the children draw pictures of themselves growing up, or have them bring pictures of what they looked like as they grew up. Instruct the children to sequence the pictures in chronological order, then have them draw pictures of what they will look like when they are adults.

4. Have the children sequence objects in graduated size (e.g., a paper clip, a pencil, a cup, a book). Or use nesting blocks and have the children sequence them from large to small, then from small to large.

A Puppy
Is a
Puppy

by _____

Nothing stays the same.

Everything can change.

A _____ is a _____

until it grows up and becomes

_____ .

A _____ is a _____

until it grows up and becomes

_____ .

puppy

kitten

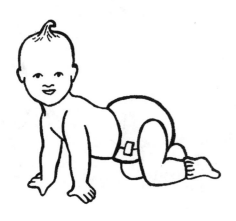

baby

cub

a dog

a cat

an adult

a bear

calf

lamb

caterpillar

tadpole

a cow

a sheep

a butterfly

a frog

202

STORY PROFILE

Guess Where You're Going,
Guess What You'll Do

Model Story: *Guess Where You're Going,*
Guess What You'll Do
by A.F. Bauman (1989)
Boston, MA: Houghton Mifflin

Description: Both words and pictures are used to create a guessing game involving familiar objects and places. Children listen for context clues and guess where they would go and what they would do in familiar places, such as at the beach, at a birthday party, on a fishing trip, at school, etc. This book has 30 pages, with five to seven sentences per page. Colorful illustrations add to the appeal of the story.

Predictable
Pattern: Guess where you're going, guess what you'll do.

Note: This story requires children to choose an illustration and then write or dictate a description of the place in the illustration. Children should write the description on the first pattern page.

For example, a child might write the following description of a farm:

There is a barn. *There are cows and horses*. *Fields of clover grow here*.

The child then glues the illustration of the farm on the next page, writing *farm* on the line below the illustration. The pattern pages are alternated this way throughout the book. Use the bottom half of page 205 as the final page of the book.

Goals:

Phonology: Reduce final consonant deletion

Reduce fronting

Produce the /g/ phoneme

Syntax: Comprehend and use verb forms (present progressive, future)

Use linguistic forms in descriptions

Thinking Skills: Draw inferences

Predict events

Make comparisons

Theme: Places to go

Additional Activities:

1. Have the children bring in objects from places they have visited. Let the other children guess the origin of the objects through a question-and-answer format.

2. Ask the children to bring in vacation photos and have them sequence the photos or tell or write a story about them.

3. Play an association game by naming items found in different places (such as the farm, the beach, the fire station, etc.) and directing the children to guess where the objects might belong.

Guess Where You're Going, Guess What You'll Do

by _____

I know where I'm going,

I know what I'll do.

_____

_____

_____

_____

(description)

Guess where you're going, guess what you'll do.

_____

(place)

the zoo

the airport

a party

school

the beach

the farm

the park

the shopping mall

208

STORY PROFILE

Who Wants One?

Model Story: ***Who Wants One?***
by Mary Serfozo (1989)
New York: Macmillan

Description: A girl, playing magician, asks her brother if he wants ONE. Despite his answer of "Yes! I want ONE!" the girl asks if he wants two, three, four, or more items. Her brother repeats his request for ONE—which turns out to be one puppy found at the end of the story. The question/answer format, rhyming, colorful illustrations, and opportunities to count to 10 make this book appealing. This 27-page book has two to four sentences per page.

Predictable Pattern: Perhaps you'll like _____.
Do you want _____? No, I want one!

Note: The pattern supplied on the bottom half of page 211 is to be used as both the second (following the title page) and the last page of this story. The mixture of digit (in the first sentence) and spelling out of the number word (in the question) is purposeful so children see both forms of the numeral.

For example:
Perhaps you'll like *2*. Do you want *two shoes*?

Goals:
Phonology: Reduce gliding
Reduce vocalization
Produce the /k/ phoneme
Produce the /t/ phoneme
Produce the /l/ phoneme

Syntax: Comprehend and use question forms (yes/no)
Comprehend and use verb forms (present, future)
Comprehend and use morphological forms (plurals)
Comprehend and use forms of negation
Comprehend and use pronouns

Semantics: Quantity concepts (numbers 1–10)

Thinking Skills: Sequence events or objects

Themes: Nature
Counting

Additional Activities:

1. Additional books to read:
   The Doorbell Rang
   by Pat Hutchins (1986)
   New York: Greenwillow Books
   Description: A large plate of cookies gets smaller and smaller as more visitors arrive at Sam and Victoria's house.

   Over in the Meadow
   by Olive A. Wadsworth (1986)
   New York: Viking Penguin
   Description: This rhyme about animals and their activities in a meadow introduces the numbers from 1–10.

2. Sing the tune "Five Little Monkeys Sitting in a Tree," changing monkeys to other animals or objects. The song is written in book form in:
   Five Little Monkeys Sitting in a Tree
   by Eileen Christelow (1991)
   New York: Houghton Mifflin

3. Collect objects on a nature walk: one nut, two leaves, etc. Make a giant collage on the bulletin board of the objects gathered. Add a written explanation of the collection (e.g., one nut, two leaves, etc.). Create a graph showing how many of each object were found.

1

Who Wants One?

by _____

Do you want 1 butterfly, 1 rainbow?
Yes, I want one!

Perhaps you'll like

_____.

(number)

Do you want

_____?

No, I want one!

Perhaps you'll like

_____.

(number)

Do you want

_____?

No, I want one!

two shoes

two eyes

three blind mice

three little pigs

**four legs
on a chair**

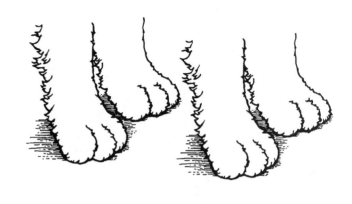

**four puppy's
paws**

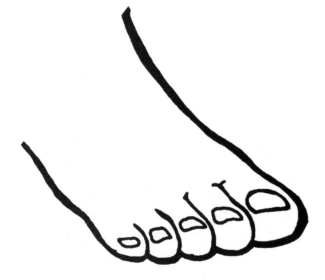

five toes

**five points
of a star**

six bees

six trees

seven jars

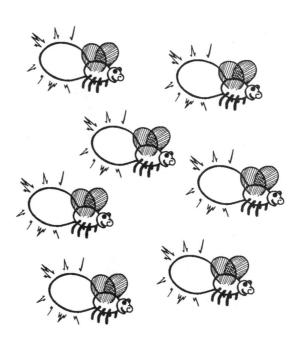

seven
lightning bugs

215

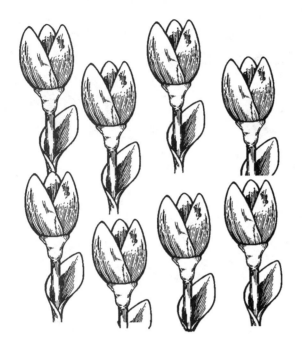

eight tulips

eight birds

nine planets

nine stars

STORY PROFILE

I Wish I Could Fly

Model Story: ***I Wish I Could Fly***
by Ron Maris (1986)
New York: Greenwillow Books

Description: A turtle wants to be like other animals who have special abilities, such as flying, running, and hopping. He realizes his own special skill of hiding in his shell to stay dry when a rainstorm comes. This book is 27 pages in length, has very large print, and uses one sentence per page. Sounds and attributes are denoted by use of all capital letters.

Predictable Pattern: I wish I could _____, but I can't _____.
I can _____.

Note: The first page of illustrations shows things that are difficult for children to do, while the second page shows things that should be easy for them to do. Alternate pages "I wish I could . . ." and "I can . . ." throughout the book. The final page can be found on the bottom half of page 219.

Goals:

Phonology: Reduce assimilation
Reduce depalatalization
Produce the /ʃ/ phoneme
Produce the /k/ phoneme

Syntax: Comprehend and use verb forms (modal)
Comprehend and use forms of negation
Comprehend and use pronouns
Comprehend and use complex sentences

Thinking Skills: Describe functions of objects
Establish causality
Make comparisons

Themes: Actions
Imagination

Additional Activities:

1. Additional book to read:
   Quick as a Cricket
   by Audrey Wood (1982)
   New York: Scholastic
   Description: This book highlights self-awareness by comparing the attributes of various animals.

2. Make an interactive language chart by writing on a large piece of tagboard various forms of the pattern phrase. Arrange the phrases, such as those following, so they are easy for children to read:

   > I wish I could _____,
   > but I can't _____.
   > I can _____.

   Direct the children, as a group, to generate responses to complete the phrases.

3. Pantomime various actions and then have the children identify the animals that could do these actions, such as:

   gallop like a horse
   hop like a bunny
   jump like a frog
   crawl like a turtle
   swim like a fish

   Let the children take turns pantomiming actions.

4. Sing and do the actions to the song "Sammy" by Hap Palmer, from the album ***Getting to Know Myself*** (Freeport, NY: Educational Activities).

I Wish I Could Fly

by _____

Right now I'm just me.
I like what I can do.

I wish I could _____,

but I can't _____.

I can _____.

drive

write

make an airplane

zip my jacket

walk

draw

make a kite

put my jacket on

tie my shoe

ride a bicycle

cross the street

ride a horse

put my shoes on

ride a tricycle

play in my yard

feed a horse

STORY PROFILE

Who Said Red?

Model Story: *Who Said Red?*
by Mary Serfozo (1988)
New York: Macmillan

Description: A girl asks a boy if he said "red." A dialogue continues about the color of various objects that are blue, yellow, green, etc., until at last the boy finds his red kite, stating, "I said red!" A question/answer format is the basis for the one to two sentences per page. This book is 28 pages long, and the sentence structure is very basic.

Predictable Pattern: Perhaps you'll like _____. (A) _____.
Do you want _____? No, I said red!

Note: The final page of this pattern book (Did you say red? A red bird, a red heart. Yes, I said red!) is supplied on the bottom half of page 227. Children should color the bird and the heart on this page red.

Goals:

Phonology: Reduce gliding
Reduce vocalization
Produce the /l/ phoneme
Produce the /r/ and semivowel /r/ phonemes

Syntax: Comprehend and use verb forms (future)
Comprehend and use question forms (yes/no)
Comprehend and use pronouns
Comprehend and use forms of negation

Semantics: Comprehend and use quality concepts (colors)

Thinking Skills: Make associations

Theme: Colors

Additional Activities:

1. Additional book to read:
   Freight Train
   by D. Crew (1978)
   New York: William Morrow
   Description: A colorful train moves through a tunnel, cities, and a trestle, then disappears.

2. Make an interactive language chart by writing on a large piece of tagboard various forms of the pattern phrase. Arrange the phrases, such as those following, so they are easy for the children to read:

   > Perhaps you'll like _____.
   > Do you want _____?
   > No, I said red!

   Direct the children, as a group, to generate responses to complete the phrases.

3. With the children, make a collage of pictures on a bulletin board with just red objects, another with just blue (or any other color) objects, etc.

4. Create a graph, such as the one following, with various color names. Color each box containing the color word. Have each child point to the box that represents the color of his or her shirt or blouse. Total the number of children wearing each particular color and graph the appropriate number.

5								
4								
3								
2								
1								
	Red	Blue	Green	Yellow	Brown	Orange	White	Purple

Who Said Red?

by _____

Did you say red?
A red bird, a red heart.

Yes, I said red!

Perhaps you'll like

_____•

(color)

_____

(color)

_____•

(object)

Do you want _____? No, I said red!

(color)

Perhaps you'll like

_____•

(color)

_____

(color)

_____•

(object)

Do you want _____? No, I said red!

(color)

A yellow
pineapple

A blue
bluejay

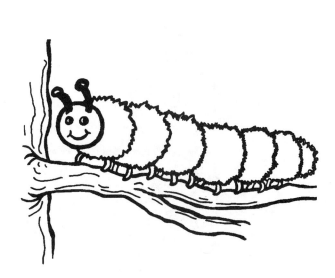

A brown
caterpillar

Green
peas

229

**Yellow
sunshine**

**Blue
blueberries**

**A brown
deer**

**A green
frog**

**Purple
grapes**

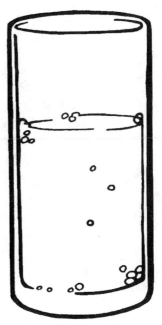

**White
milk**

**Orange
pumpkins**

**A black
bat**

A purple flower

White clouds

Orange oranges

A black hat

STORY PROFILES

Have You Seen My Toy?
Have You Seen My Pet?

Model Story: *Have You Seen My Cat?*
by Eric Carle (1987)
Natick, MA: Picture Book Studio

Description: A boy asks, "Have you seen my cat?" and is pointed in the direction of several large cats, such as a lion, a tiger, and a panther. Finally, someone points to a cat hiding in a park. This is the boy's cat . . . and now she has kittens! A very simple sentence structure in a question/answer format is the basis for this book. There is a great deal of repetition throughout the book, with one sentence per page. Very colorful illustrations enhance this 21-page story.

Predictable Patterns: Have you seen my toy/pet?
This _____ is not my toy/pet!

Note: The final pages of each of these pattern books are supplied on the bottom halves of pages 236 and 240. Children are encouraged to draw their own toys/pets on the final page.

Goals:

Phonology: Reduce final consonant deletion
Reduce stopping
Produce /s/ and /z/ phonemes
Produce the /ð/ phoneme
Produce the /v/ phoneme
Produce the /m/ and /p/ phonemes
Produce the /t/ phoneme

Syntax: Comprehend and use verb forms (copula)
Comprehend and use question forms (yes/no)
Comprehend and use pronouns
Comprehend and use forms of negation

Semantics: Comprehend and use quality concepts (colors)

Thinking Skills: Categorize objects

Themes: Toys
Animals

Additional Activities:

1. Additional books to read:

   The Very Hungry Caterpillar
   by Eric Carle (1987)
   New York: Putnam
   Description: A caterpillar eats its way through various foods, increasing the number of the items each day of the week. The pages contain holes where the caterpillar eats through them.

   Use the pattern phrase: On <u>(day of the week)</u>, it ate through _____.

   Any Kind of Dog
   by Lynn Reiser (1992)
   New York: Greenwillow Books
   Description: A child wants a pet dog, even after his mother tries to give him other kinds of pets.

2. Play the game "I Spy." Have a child pick something in the room and then describe it to the other children. Instruct the other children to guess what the object is.

   For example:

   I see something that can be written on, but you can't use a pencil to write on it. Teachers use it a lot to write on with chalk. (It's a chalkboard.)

3. Make masks that look like the children's pets. Using paper bags, cut out the eyes, nose, and mouth for each pet. Have the children draw the heads of their pets on their bags. They can also use yarn for fur, construction paper for scales, etc.

4. Tell the children to draw pictures of their favorite toys. Let each child share information about why he or she likes the toy, where the toy came from, etc.

Have You Seen My Toy?

by _____

Have you seen my toy?

This is my toy!

It's a

_____.

Have you seen my toy?

This _____ is not my toy!

Have you seen my toy?

This _____ is not my toy!

truck

doll

bicycle

coloring book

teddy bear

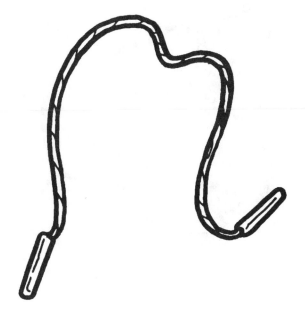

jump rope

puzzle

ball

Have You Seen My Pet?

by _____

Have you seen my pet?

This is my pet!

It's a

_____.

Have you seen my pet?

This _____ is not my pet!

Have you seen my pet?

This _____ is not my pet!

bird

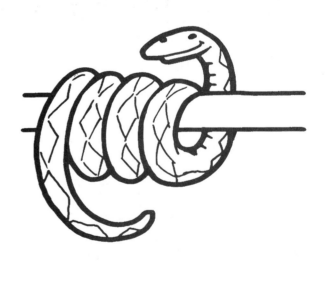

dog

cat

snake

rabbit

frog

turtle

hamster

Don't Climb out of the Window Tonight

Model Story: **_Don't Climb out of the Window Tonight_**
by Richard McGilvray (1993)
New York: Dial Books

Description: A little girl gives reasons why she should not climb out her window at night. Reasons involve various monsters that are whimsically illustrated. In the end, she falls asleep counting monsters. This book includes 24 pages with one partial sentence in large print per page (e.g., "Don't climb out of the window tonight because . . ." on one page and the reason on the next page).

Predictable Pattern: Don't climb out of the window tonight because _____.

Note: On the blank lines of the pattern pages, children write their predictions of what each object illustrated is doing outside (e.g., the spider is spinning a web on my window). The final page of this story can be found on the bottom half of page 246. The children draw themselves in bed on this page.

Goals:

Phonology: Reduce final consonant deletion
Reduce cluster simplification
Produce the /ð/ phoneme
Produce the /t/ and /d/ phonemes

Syntax: Comprehend and use forms of negation
Comprehend and use complex sentence structure
Comprehend and use verb forms (present)

Semantics: Comprehend and use time concepts (tonight)
Comprehend and use spatial concepts (out)

Thinking Skills: Predict events
Establish causality

Themes: Imagination
Nature
Time

Additional Activities:

1. Additional book to read:
   Where the Wild Things Are
   by Maurice Sendak (1964)
   New York: Harper and Row
   Description: In this story, a little boy who misbehaved is sent to his room, where he dreams of a lunch with "wild things."

2. Let children draw anything pertaining to Halloween. Allow them to use their imaginations and then have them describe their pictures to each other.

3. Use the following pattern in a safety lesson using rules such as:

   Don't touch the hot stove because _____.
   Don't touch the wall outlets because _____.
   Don't swim by yourself because _____.
   Don't talk to strangers because _____.

4. Expand the pattern phrase to incorporate weather words and descriptions, such as:

   Don't climb out of the window tonight because (*rain is dripping off the roof*).

   Don't climb out of the window tonight because (a *tornado is swirling around in the fields*).

   Don't climb out of the window tonight because (*lightning is flashing in the sky*).

5. With the children, generate a list of good things that happen at night:

   You get sleep so you feel rested.
   You cool down after a hot day.
   The stars come out.
   You can look at the moon.

Don't Climb out of the Window Tonight

by _____

Don't climb out of the window tonight. Stay in your nice, warm bed.

**Don't climb out
of the window
tonight because**

_____

_____

_____ .

**Don't climb out
of the window
tonight because**

_____

_____

_____ .

the ghost

the pumpkin

the full moon

the skeleton

the black cat

the witch

the bat

the spider

Sitting in My Tent
Sitting in My Spaceship

Model Story: *Sitting in My Box*
by Dee Lillegard (1989)
New York: Dutton

Description: A boy is alone, sitting in a box, until a variety of animals ask if they can join him. Soon the box becomes too crowded, but none of the animals are willing to leave. Just then, a flea jumps into the box, making all of the animals "flee"! The boy is alone in his box again, this time with a book about wild animals. Discussion of what is real and what is pretend can be a major focus when using this book. This 27-page book contains one to three sentences per page.

Predictable Pattern: A _____ knocks. "Let me, let me in." So I move over. No more room! Out goes the _____.

Note: The sequence of the book is as follows:

1. "I'm sitting in my (tent/spaceship) alone," is the second pattern page (following the title page).

2. "A _____ knocks. 'Let me, let me in.' So I move over." (This page is repeated until all of the animals/objects are in the tent/spaceship.)

3. "No more room! Out goes the _____." (This page is repeated until all of the animals/objects are out of the tent/spaceship.)

4. "I'm sitting in my tent/spaceship alone," is the last page.

Children are required to generate their own size adjectives (e.g., big, huge, large, teeny-weeny, little, etc.).

Children should draw themselves in the tent or in the spaceship on the second page and the last page (the bottom halves of pages 253 and 257) of these stories.

Goals:

Phonology: Reduce gliding

Reduce final consonant deletion

Reduce cluster simplification

Reduce fronting

Produce the /r/ and semivowel /r/ phonemes

Produce the /l/ phoneme

Produce the /g/ phoneme

Produce the /s/ and /z/ phonemes

Produce the /v/ phoneme

Syntax: Comprehend and use verb forms (present)

Comprehend and use pronouns

Semantics: Comprehend and use spatial concepts (in/out, over)

Comprehend and use quality concepts (size)

Thinking Skills: Make comparisons

Establish causality

Sequence events

Themes: Places to go

Nature

Imagination

Additional Activities: 1. Make an interactive language chart by writing on a large piece of tagboard various forms of the pattern phrase. Arrange the phrases, such as those following, so they are easy for the children to read:

> A _____ knocks.
> "Let me, let me in."
> So I move over.
> No more room!
> Out goes the _____.

Direct the children, as a group, to generate responses to complete the phrases.

2. Play a memory game with the children. After reading the model story, have the children draw or write all of the objects they can remember that went in and out of the box. Talk about objects each child remembered and which objects they forgot.

3. Set up a make-believe tent (e.g., using a blanket to cover a table) or decorate a large appliance box so that children can act out the story. Use real objects, stuffed animals, or the illustrations as props.

4. Instead of using size words, use other quality concepts (adjectives) to describe the animals or objects, such as:

sneaky bear	green planet
grumpy lion	intelligent astronaut
nervous bird	unusual Martian
sleepy elephant	powerful telescope
tired ant	shooting star
busy squirrel	flying comet
lazy dinosaur	floating space station
friendly fox	bright sun

5. Collect boxes of various sizes. Allow the children to try to guess what could fit in each. Collect various items so that the children can try to fit objects into the different boxes (e.g., a flat, thin box is usually a glove, tie, or scarf box).

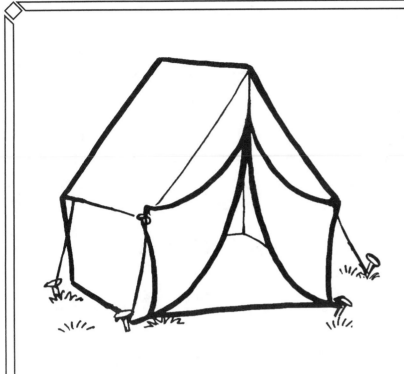

Sitting in My Tent

by _____

I'm sitting in my tent alone.

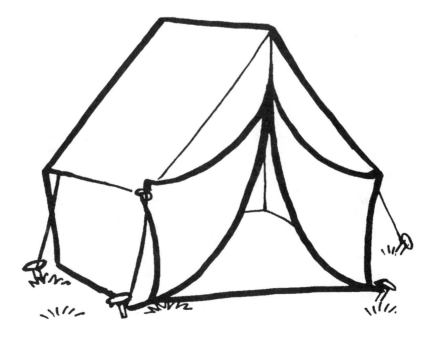

A _____
(size)

_____
(object)

knocks.

"Let me, let me in."

So I move over.

No more room!

Out goes the

_____ .

bear

lion

bird

elephant

ant

squirrel

dinosaur

fox

Sitting
in My
Spaceship

by _____

I'm sitting in my spaceship alone.

257

A _____
(size)

_____
(object)

knocks.

"Let me, let me in."

So I move over.

No more room!

Out goes the

_____.

planet

astronaut

Martian

telescope

star

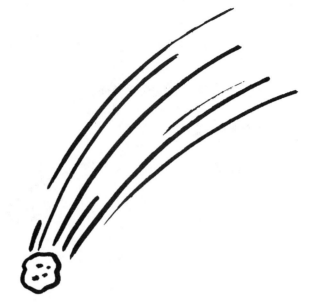

comet

space station

sun

STORY PROFILE

These Are My Pets

Model Story: ***Little Critter's These Are My Pets***
by Mercer Mayer (1988)
Racine, WI: Western Publishing

Description: Various pets are collected by a young child. Pets are described by color and by action words (flying, jumping, running, etc.). The child likes to do what the pets can do as they play together all day. Each of this story's 31 pages has two to three simple sentences and large print.

Predictable Pattern: This is my _____.
My _____ likes to _____.
My _____ is my friend.

Note: The children should write the animal name after each "my" on the pattern page, then, fill in the blank with the activity that the animal likes to do. The bottom half of page 263 is the final page of the book. The children should count the pets in their books when completed.

Goals:
Phonology: Reduce cluster simplification
Reduce final consonant deletion
Reduce gliding
Reduce assimilation
Produce the /ð/ phoneme
Produce the /s/ and /z/ phonemes
Produce the /m/ phoneme
Produce the /l/ phoneme
Produce the /t/ phoneme

Syntax: Comprehend and use verb forms (present, copula)
Comprehend and use pronouns

Semantics: Comprehend and use quality concepts (numbers 1–10)

Thinking Skills: Make associations
Describe functions of objects

Themes: Animals
Actions
Counting

Additional Activities:

1. Tell each child to bring in a stuffed animal. Have each child describe his or her stuffed animal to the other children.

2. Make a graph of the children's pets such as the one following:

5						
4						
3						
2						
1						
	Dog	Cat	Gerbil	Hamster	Bird	Fish

Talk about the activities each pet can do and how the various pets are the same and different.

3. Take a field trip to the pet store or hold "Pet Day" and let each child bring a pet to school. After the trip or visit, have each child draw a picture of one of the animals. Then have the children write or dictate stories about the animals, including the activities of the animals and how they would have to be taken care of.

4. Expand the pattern phrase to incorporate family members and their activities, such as:

This is my dad.
My dad likes to cook.
My dad is my friend.

These Are
My Pets

by _____

These are my pets.
These are my friends.

This is my

_____ .
(animal)

My _____ likes to _____ .
(animal)   (action)

My _____ is my friend.
(animal)

This is my

_____ .
(animal)

My _____ likes to _____ .
(animal)   (action)

My _____ is my friend.
(animal)

bird

dog

cat

snake

rabbit

frog

turtle

hamster

STORY PROFILE

Hide and Snake

Model Story: *Hide and Snake*
by Keith Baker (1991)
New York: Harcourt, Brace, Jovanovich

Description: A snake plays hide-and-seek with the readers of this book. The snake slithers into and around a variety of colorful objects—almost (but not quite) disappearing from view. One phrase per page and very large print make this book appealing to a variety of reading levels. The total length of the book is 29 pages; however, many of the pages do not have text—they are entirely illustrations.

Predictable Pattern: Where's the snake?
I found the snake.
He's hiding _____.

Note: Encourage children to use their imaginations in choosing hiding places for the snake. The bottom half of page 269 provides the final page for the book. Children can draw a happy snake on this page if they want to.

Goals:

Phonology: Reduce final consonant deletion
Reduce assimilation
Reduce cluster simplification
Reduce stopping
Produce the /z/ phoneme
Produce the /k/ phoneme
Produce the /f/ phoneme

Syntax: Comprehend and use question forms (where)
Comprehend and use pronouns

Comprehend and use verb forms (present progressive, copula, past)

Use linguistic forms in descriptions

Semantics: Comprehend and use spatial concepts (behind, on, in, above/below, next to, around, under)

Thinking Skills: Make comparisons

Themes: Animals
Nature
Imagination

Additional Activities:

1. Additional books to read:

    In the Tall, Tall Grass
    by Denise Fleming (1991)
    New York: Holt
    Description: A caterpillar crawls through the tall grass, looking at several busy animals. Various animal camouflages are shown.

    Who's Hiding Here?
    by Yoshi Pitt (1987)
    New York: Putnam
    Description: Through rhyme and riddle, children are introduced to camouflage and mimicry in nature.

2. Discuss other animals and places where they can hide, such as a squirrel in a tree, a bear in a cave, or a groundhog in a hole in the ground.

3. Have the children observe the activities of an animal in the classroom, such as a turtle, gerbil, or rabbit. As a group, make an observation log of the activities of the animal.

4. Let children share stories of items (or even pets) they have lost and how or where they finally found them.

Hide and Snake

by _____

I found the snake every time!

Where's the
snake?

I found the snake.

He's hiding _____.

Where's the
snake?

I found the snake.

He's hiding _____.

behind a tree

in a hole

**under a
bird house**

**on top of a
stop sign**

271

below a swing

next to a cactus

around a ladder

above my window

STORY PROFILE

Who Sank the Boat?

Model Story: *Who Sank the Boat?*
by Pamela Allen (1982)
New York: Coward-McCaan

Description: A group of farm animals attempts to take a trip in a boat. The boat gets overloaded and sinks, but who sank the boat? The smallest animal of all—a mouse! This story has one to two sentences per page and a question/answer format. Both simple and complex sentences make up the story in this 26-page book. Large print makes reading easier for many children.

**Predictable
Pattern:** Did the _____ sink the boat? No, it wasn't the _____ who sank the boat. Do you know who sank the boat?

Note: The final page of this story can be found on the bottom half of page 275.

Goals:
Phonology: Reduce cluster simplification
Reduce final consonant deletion
Reduce stopping
Produce the /s/ phoneme
Produce the /b/ phoneme
Produce the /d/ and /t/ phonemes
Produce the /ð/ phoneme

Syntax: Comprehend and use verb forms (past)
Comprehend and use morphological forms (articles)
Comprehend and use question forms (yes/no)

273

Comprehend and use complex sentence structures

Comprehend and use forms of negation

Semantics: Comprehend and use quality concepts (size—smaller than, larger than)

Thinking Skills: Predict events

Make comparisons

Sequence events or objects

Themes: Animals

Nature

Actions

Additional Activities:

1. Additional book to read:

   A Lion in the Night

   by Pamela Allen (1985)

   New York: Putnam

   Description: A royal household is disrupted when a lion runs off with the baby.

2. Gather objects of varying size (e.g., dime, watch, block, plate). Have the children sequence objects by size (e.g., dime, watch, block, plate). Use actual or miniature objects that are in size relation. Then extend the sequences to pictures of objects.

3. Allow children to experiment with various weighted objects in a large tub of water to see if they sink or float.

4. Using a balance scale, let children make weight comparisons of various objects. Direct them to determine which object is heavier and which is lighter.

5. Present children with pictures of various forms of transportation. Give the children choices pertaining to size, such as:

   Could an elephant fit in a rowboat or a cargo ship?

   Could a lion fit in the back of your car or a pickup truck?

Who Sank the Boat?

by _____

Did the _____ sink the boat?

Yes, the

_____

sank the boat!

Did the

_____

sink the boat?

No, it wasn't the

_____

who sank the boat.

Do you know who sank the boat?

Did the

_____

sink the boat?

No, it wasn't the

_____

who sank the boat.

Do you know who sank the boat?

ant

woodpecker

turtle

monkey

beaver

gorilla

giraffe

elephant

Dear Department Store
Dear Restaurant

Model Story: *Dear Zoo*
by Rod Campbell (1982)
New York: Four Winds Press

Description: In response to a request for a pet, the zoo sends a variety of animals in a variety of containers. (This book contains pop-up pictures of the animals in their containers.) None of the animals turn out to be the desired pet, until the zoo sends a puppy. This 16-page book has large text, with one to two sentences per page. Animal descriptions are provided, such as *too big, too tall, too grumpy,* etc.

Predictable Patterns: I called the department store to send me a present.
They sent me _____.
It was/They were too _____, so I sent it/them back!

I went to the restaurant to order some dinner.
They gave me _____.
It was/They were too _____, so I sent it/them back!

Note: The final pages of each of these stories can be found on the bottom halves of pages 282 and 286. Children fill in the blank with their own ideas on these pages.

In the department store and restaurant illustrations, the words in parentheses are the suggested reasons for sending the objects or items back. Children write this reason (or a reason they have thought of) on the blank lines or they can dictate the reason for adults to write.

Goals:

Phonology: Reduce weak syllable deletion
Reduce cluster simplification
Reduce vocalization
Reduce fronting
Produce the /s/ and /z/ phonemes
Produce the /k/ and /g/ phonemes
Produce the /ð/ phoneme
Produce the /r/ and semivowel /r/ phonemes
Produce the /t/ and /d/ phonemes

Syntax: Comprehend and use complex sentence structures
Comprehend and use verb forms (past)
Comprehend and use pronouns
Use linguistic forms in descriptions

Semantics: Comprehend and use quality concepts (size, misc.)

Thinking Skills: Make associations
Make comparisons
Establish causality

Theme: Places to go

Additional Activities:

1. Additional book to read:
   The Jolly Postman
   by Janet and Allen Ahlberg (1986)
   Boston, MA: Little, Brown
   Description: A series of letters are delivered to folk and fairy tale characters. Letters can be taken out of envelopes attached to the book.

2. Help each child write a letter to a child in another class telling about himself or herself.

3. Help the children make telephone calls to ask for information (e.g., ask a store when it is open, ask a pizza place what size pizzas it has).

4. Make an interactive language chart by writing on a large piece of tagboard various forms of the pattern phrase. Arrange the phrases, such as those following, so they are easy to read:

> I called the department store
> to send me a present.
> They sent me _____.
> It was too _____,
> so I sent it back.

> I went to the restaurant
> to order some dinner.
> They gave me _____.
> It was too _____,
> so I sent it back.

Direct the children, as a group, to generate responses to complete the phrases.

5. Gather pictures of objects children could categorize by different kinds of stores. Decorate file folders to represent a grocery store, clothing store, pet store, and toy store. Include pictures of things that would be found in each store. Have the children sort the items associated with each store and then put them in the correct folders.

6. Ask a local restaurant (where you know children eat) if you can have a menu. Find out what the children like and dislike and their reasons.

Dear Department Store

by _____

I called the

department store to

send me a present.

They sent me

_____.

I kept it!

I called the
department store to
send me a present.
They sent me

_____.

It was too _____,
(reason)

so I sent it back!

I called the
department store to
send me a present.
They sent me

_____.

They were too _____,
(reason)

so I sent them back!

**a pair of shoes
(little)**

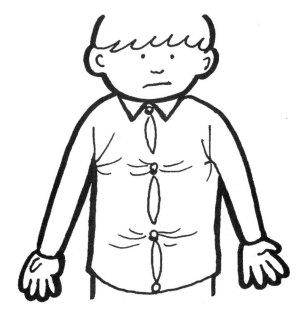

**a shirt
(tight)**

**a blanket
(scratchy)**

**a TV
(blurry)**

**a ring
(dull)**

**a suitcase
(small)**

**a refrigerator
(warm)**

**a radio
(loud)**

Dear Restaurant

by _____

I went to the restaurant to order some dinner. They gave me

_____ .

I kept it!

I went to the restaurant to order some dinner. They gave me

_____

_____.

It was too _____, so I sent it back!
(reason)

I went to the restaurant to order some dinner. They gave me

_____

_____.

They were too

_____,
(reason)

so I sent them back!

chili
(spicy)

spaghetti
(long)

soup
(salty)

peanut butter
and jelly (sticky)

**bananas
(mushy)**

**ice cream
(cold)**

**milk
(sour)**

**french fries
(crunchy)**

 **STORY PROFILE**

I Went Walking

Model Story: *I Went Walking*
by Sue Williams (1989)
New York: Harcourt, Brace, Jovanovich

Description: A boy goes walking and responds to the question "What did you see?" by describing the many animals he sees on his outing. The animals follow him one by one to the end of the story. This 28-page book contains very large print, one sentence per page, and a very simple, repetitive sentence structure.

Predictable Pattern: I went walking.
Who did you see?
I saw _____ looking at me.

Note: Illustrations on pages 294 and 296 show objects related to specific occupations. Have the children glue these objects onto the page with the pattern phrase, "I went walking. Who did you see?" The object names are not written on the pattern pages; the illustrations simply add interest to these pages.

Illustrations on pages 295 and 297 show the persons associated with the objects. Children should glue these illustrations onto the pattern page that reads, "I saw _____ looking at me." Alternate these two pattern pages throughout the book.

The final page of the book is on the bottom half of page 292.

290

Goals:

Phonology: Reduce gliding
Reduce stopping
Reduce depalatalization
Produce the /s/ phoneme
Produce the /l/ phoneme

Syntax: Comprehend and use question forms (who)
Comprehend and use morphological forms (articles)
Comprehend and use verb forms (past)
Comprehend and use pronouns

Thinking Skills: Make associations
Predict events

Theme: People (jobs)

Additional Activities:

1. Take an imaginary trip through the forest or desert. Use the pattern phrase substituting the word *what* for *who*. (E.g., I went walking. What did you see? I saw a tree looking at me.)

2. Have each child bring a tool or item related to his or her parent's or caregiver's job and have the other children guess what type of work the adult does. Have children use the pattern phrase, "My dad/mom uses _____ at his/her job. My dad/mom is a/an _____."

3. Help children to name a few endangered animals. Identify on a map the countries where the endangered animals live. Have the children name some characteristics of the animals (e.g., a whale lives in the ocean, blows out water, and is very big).

4. To gain awareness of surroundings, have students take a walk on a frequently traveled path or sidewalk and note things and sounds around them. Then take them on a walk somewhere new (in the park, on a new trail, behind the school, etc.) and note similarities to and differences from the first walk.

I Went Walking

by _____

I met the people who work
in my neighborhood.

I went walking.
Who did you see?

I saw _____ looking at me.

hammer and nails

scissors

stethoscope

mixer and bowl

a builder

a hairdresser

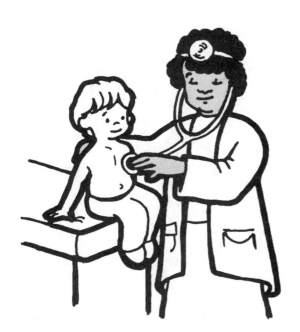

a doctor

a baker

letters

toothbrush

badge

book and chalkboard

a mail carrier

a dentist

a police officer

a teacher

STORY PROFILE

This Is What I'll Wear

Model Story: ***The Dress I'll Wear to the Party***
by Shirley Neitzel (1992)
New York: Greenwillow Books

Description: A girl describes the clothes she will wear to a party as she dresses up in her mother's clothing and jewelry. The rhythm of this story follows the famous book, "The House that Jack Built." Pictures of the clothing items are used in place of words in the sentences of this book. Sentence structure is basic but contains some compound and complex elements. This 29-page story has very large print.

Predictable Pattern: This is the _____ that I'll use for _____.

Note: Children select and glue two illustrations per page in this pattern book (one illustration of sports equipment or clothes, and one illustration of the associated sport). The last page of the book can be found on the bottom half of page 300. On this page, children draw themselves wearing attire from their favorite sport. The blank line is filled in with a verb and the sport (e.g., play football, go swimming).

Goals:

Phonology: Reduce stopping
Produce the /l/ phoneme
Produce the /s/ and /z/ phonemes
Produce the /ð/ phoneme

Syntax: Comprehend and use verb forms (copula, future)
Comprehend and use pronouns

298

Comprehend and use morphological forms (articles)
Comprehend and use complex sentences

Thinking Skills: Make associations
Draw inferences
Categorize objects

Theme: People (sports)

Additional Activities:

1. Additional book to read:

   The Jacket I Wear in the Snow
   by Shirley Neitzel (1989)
   New York: Greenwillow Books
   Description: A little boy wants to go out in the snow, so he has to put on layers of clothing to keep warm.

2. Ask children "what if" questions, such as:

   What if you didn't wear a helmet while playing football? What might happen?

   What if you didn't have a hockey stick to play hockey? What would you use?

   What if you didn't have a mitt to play baseball? What might happen?

   What if you didn't have a basketball hoop to play basketball? What else could you use?

3. Have the children tell the sequence of how they get ready for school in the morning. Use the pattern phrases:

   This is the _____ I'll wear to school.

   This is the _____ I'll take to school.

4. Make a song to go with the sequence of dressing for school in the morning. This will serve as a memory cue for some children who have a hard time getting ready for school in a timely manner.

This Is What I'll Wear

by _____

This is what I look like

when I _____.

This is the _____
(equipment/clothes)

that I'll use for _____.
(sport)

This is the _____
(equipment/clothes)

that I'll use for _____.
(sport)

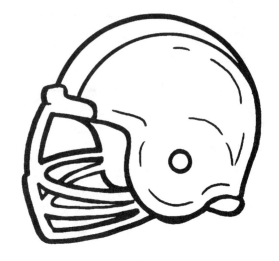

helmet

glove

jersey

stick

302

football

baseball

basketball

ice hockey

uniform

ball

pair of skates

bathing suit

baseball

soccer

street hockey

swimming

 **STORY PROFILE**

This Is the Bunny

Model Story: *This Is the Bear*
by Sarah Hayes (1986)
New York: Lippincott

Description: A dog accidentally pushes a teddy bear into a garbage can, and the bear gets taken to the city dump. The bear's owner, a young boy, searches for him at the dump with the assistance of a grouchy garbage collector. The bear is found and returns home to tell the other toys of his adventure. This 24-page book has simple sentence structure, with one to two sentences per page and large print.

**Predictable
Pattern:** This is the bunny who goes to the _____.

Note: The final page of this story is supplied on the bottom of page 308.

Goals:
Phonology: Reduce final consonant deletion
Reduce weak syllable deletion
Produce the /s/ and /z/ phonemes
Produce the /b/ phoneme
Produce the /ð/ phoneme

Syntax: Comprehend and use morphological forms (articles)
Comprehend and use verb forms (copula, present)
Comprehend and use complex sentences

Thinking Skills: Make associations
Predict events
Draw inferences

Themes: Places to go
Actions

**Additional
Activities:**

1. Additional books to read:
   This Is the Bear and the Picnic Lunch
   by Sarah Hayes (1988)
   Cambridge, MA: Candlewick Press
   Description: A boy and a teddy bear's picnic still takes place even though a dog tries to stop them.

   Corduroy
   by Don Freeman (1983)
   New York: Penguin Books
   Description: A stuffed bear waiting hopefully in a toy department finds a home with a girl who wants him so much that when her mother refuses to buy the bear, the little girl buys him with her own money.

2. Take the children on a walk in their community and identify the businesses and the services they provide.

3. Make a sequence story by forming associations similar to those in ***If You Give a Mouse a Cookie*** (see page 177). (For example, you go to the bank to get some cash. Then you go to the department store to buy clothes, which will remind you to go to the dry cleaner to pick up your clothes there. After picking up the clothes, you see a restaurant and you want to eat dinner, which reminds you that you need to go to the grocery store to buy food, and then you will need more money.)

4. With the students, make a "Community Helpers" chart that lists the helpers and their roles in the community (e.g., police to protect, sanitation workers to collect trash).

This Is the Bunny

by _____

This is the bunny who comes home to hug me.

This is the bunny

who goes to the

_____

_____

_____.

(place)

This is the bunny

who goes to the

_____

_____

_____.

(place)

grocery store
to buy food

bank
to cash a check

post office
to mail a letter

department store
to buy clothes

310

**gas station
to pump gas**

**dry cleaner
to pick up clothes**

**barber to
get a haircut**

**restaurant
to buy dinner**

Here Comes a Bus

Model Story: *Here Comes a Bus*
by Harriet Ziefert (1988)
New York: Penguin Books

Description: A girl and boy are waiting at the bus stop for the bus to the park. Several buses bound for other places, including a zoo, farm, aquarium, dog show, and museum, stop before the right bus comes along. The book length is 15 pages. The pattern phrase is repeated on each page, then a flap opens on a bus to reveal various animals and where they are from. This book has short and simple sentences in large print.

**Predictable
Pattern:** Look! Look! Here comes _____.
Could this be for us?
No, it's _____. We want a bus.

Note: The final page for this story is supplied on the bottom half of page 314. Children should draw a picture of a bus to match the text.

Goals:

Phonology: Reduce fronting
Reduce gliding
Produce the /k/ and /g/ phonemes
Produce the /s/ and /z/ phonemes
Produce the /l/ phoneme
Produce the /b/ phoneme

Syntax: Comprehend and use question forms (yes/no)
Comprehend and use morphological forms (articles)

Comprehend and use verb forms (present, copula, modal)
Comprehend and use pronouns
Comprehend and use forms of negation

Thinking Skills: Make associations
Categorize objects
Draw inferences

Theme: Imagination

Additional Activities:

1. Additional book to read:

   The Wheels on the Bus
   by Maryann Kovalski (1987)
   Boston, MA: Little, Brown
   Description: This book provides the text and illustrations for the classic children's song "The Wheels on the Bus."

2. Discuss the following ideas:

   Why people use a taxi
   Why people use a jeep
   Why people use a tow truck
   Why people use an ambulance

3. With the children, make a bus out of an appliance box. Paint it yellow (or decorate it with yellow paper) and put wheels, windows, and lights on the bus. Allow children to sit in the bus while they read their stories to one another.

4. Collect pictures of various forms of transportation. Help children to compare them in size, shape, color, number of wheels, and other aspects.

Here Comes a Bus

by _____

Look! Look! Here comes a bus.
Could this be for us?

Yes, it's a bus!

Look! Look!

Here comes

_____ .

Could this be for us?

No, it's

_____ .

We want a bus.

Look! Look!

Here comes

_____ .

Could this be for us?

No, it's

_____ .

We want a bus.

a taxi

a jeep

a tractor

a fire engine

a garbage truck

a police car

a tow truck

an ambulance

STORY PROFILES

The Mouse Book
The Elephant Book

Model Story: These pattern books were developed for remediation by Robin Peura.

Predictable Patterns:

_____ is larger than a mouse.

_____ is smaller than a mouse.

_____ is larger than an elephant.

_____ is smaller than an elephant.

Note: Alternate pattern pages of "larger than a mouse" and "smaller than a mouse" in *The Mouse Book*. Alternate pattern pages of "larger than an elephant" and "smaller than an elephant" in *The Elephant Book*. Provide illustrations from pages 322–323 and 326–327 for both books so children can choose the appropriate illustration to fit the phrase.

The final pages of the books are on the bottom halves of pages 320 and 324. Have the children complete the sentence with the word *larger* or *smaller,* as appropriate. They can then draw a picture showing the size difference between themselves and the mouse (or the elephant).

Goals:

Phonology: Reduce weak syllable deletion

Reduce gliding

Reduce cluster simplification

Reduce vocalization

Produce the /m/ phoneme

Produce the /z/ phoneme

Produce the /l/ phoneme

Produce the /ð/ phoneme

Syntax: Comprehend and use verb forms (copula)
Comprehend and use morphological forms (articles)
Comprehend and use complex sentence structures

Semantics: Comprehend and use quality concepts (size—smaller than/larger than)

Thinking Skills: Make comparisons

Theme: Animals

Additional Activities:

1. Additional books to read:
   Is It Larger? Is It Smaller?
   by Tana Hoban (1985)
   New York: Greenwillow Books
   Description: A wordless book that depicts the concept of size through color photos of objects.

   The Three Bears
   by Paul Galdone (1984)
   New York: Scholastic
   Description: This classic tale of Goldilock's visit to the home of the three bears provides opportunities for sequencing objects by size.

2. Collect objects or pictures of objects of various sizes. Determine if the objects are or might be larger than an elephant, smaller than an elephant, larger than a mouse, and smaller than a mouse. Use other animals for the comparison (e.g., smaller than a bee, larger than a bee, etc.).

3. Give the children several pictures of animals. Direct them to sequence the pictures according to the size of the animals (e.g., elephant, gorilla, raccoon, hamster).

4. Visit a zoo and compare animal sizes.

The Mouse Book

by _____

I am _____ than a
mouse, and I like that size!

_____ **is larger than a mouse.**

_____ **is smaller than a mouse.**

An ant

A penny

A key

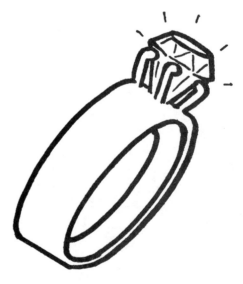

A ring

322

A pin

An eraser

A crayon

An M & M

The Elephant Book

by _____

I am _____ than an elephant, and I like that size!

_____

is larger than an elephant.

_____

is smaller than an elephant.

A building

A house

A store

The earth

The sun

A mountain

A plane

A semi-truck

STORY PROFILE

How Do You Know?

Model Story: This pattern book was developed for remediation by Robin Peura.

Predictable Pattern: How do you know that someone is _____?
I know because _____.

Note: This ***Story Making*** pattern book requires children to write or dictate descriptions of various emotions or actions. Children should fill in the first blank with an emotion or action and then give the description in the space provided after "because" on the pattern page.

The bottom half of page 330 contains the final page of the book. Children should fill in the first blank with an emotion or action, give a description after "because," and then draw a picture of themselves. (Children may dictate their responses to an adult rather than writing.)

Goals:
Phonology: Reduce final consonant deletion
Reduce stopping
Produce the /s/ and /z/ phonemes
Produce the /d/ phoneme
Produce the /ð/ phoneme
Produce the /b/ phoneme

Syntax: Comprehend and use question forms (how)
Comprehend and use pronouns
Comprehend and use verb forms (present, present progressive, future)
Comprehend and use complex sentence stuctures

Thinking Skills: Make comparisons
Draw inferences

Themes: People (feelings)
Actions
Imagination

**Additional
Activities:**
1. Additional book to read:
   ***Alexander and the Terrible, Horrible, No Good,
   Very Bad Day***
   by Judith Viorst (1976)
   New York: Macmillan
   Description: This book describes the terrible, horrible, no good situations that make a very bad day for Alexander.

2. Demonstrate feelings using body language and have the children guess which emotion is indicated by the body language. Have them predict why they may be feeling that way.

3. Using rebus symbols (or pictographs) that represent feelings, have the children fill in the pattern phrase:

   I am _____ when _____.
   ___(feeling)___

4. Have the children draw things that happen on a good day and on a bad day. Then have the children explain or describe each picture.

How Do You Know?

by _____

You'll know that I am _____

because _____

_____.

How do you know

that someone is

_____?

I know because _____

_____.

How do you know

that someone is

_____?

I know because _____

_____.

sad

happy

angry

nervous

frightened

embarrassed

bored

confused

333

cooking

sewing

running

reading

sleeping

writing

crying

watching TV

STORY PROFILE

Where's the Dinosaur?

Model Story: This pattern book was developed for remediation by Robin Peura.

Predictable Pattern: Where's the dinosaur? _____.

Note: Children cut out the small dinosaur from the bottom of page 338 and color it. The dinosaur is attached to the cover of the book with a long piece of yarn. After punching a hole at the top of the title page and in the dinosaur, tie the ends of the long piece of yarn to each.

Make one copy of each page (pages 339–347) for each child, cut them apart, and bind the pages to make a book. Page 347 should be filled in as each child wishes with a location and an object. Illustrations from elsewhere in the book could be used on this page (e.g., on top of a penny, under the stick). On each page, have children mark an X in the spot where the dinosaur should be on that page. When reading the book, the small dinosaur tied to the book with a long string might be placed over the X on each page.

Goals:
Phonology: Reduce weak syllable deletion
Reduce vocalization
Produce the /d/ phoneme
Produce the /s/ phoneme
Produce the /ð/ phoneme

Syntax: Comprehend and use question forms (where)
Comprehend and use verb forms (copula)
Comprehend and use morphological forms (articles)

Semantics: Comprehend and use spatial concepts (on, beside, between, under, over, in front of/in back of, up/down, inside/outside)

Theme: Animals

Additional Activities:

1. Additional books to read:

   We're Going on a Bear Hunt
   by M. Rosen and H. Oxenbury (1989)
   New York: Macmillan
   Description: This story tells of the exciting adventure of a family that treks over hill and dale to find a bear and then narrowly escapes danger when they find one!

   Going on a Lion Hunt
   by H. Ziefert and M. Smith (1989)
   New York: Puffin Books
   Description: A child leaves home in pursuit of a lion and goes through a varied terrain, only to be frightened by the lion and return through the terrain to his home.

   Rosie's Walk
   by Pat Hutchins (1987)
   New York: Scholastic
   Description: Rosie, a hen, walks around the farmyard trailed by a fox who has a series of mishaps (illustrated by pictures) that allow Rosie to walk safely back home.

2. Make a diarama out of a shoebox. Include representations of trees, plants, rocks, and water. Move dinosaurs to various places and have the children tell where they are using spatial concepts (e.g., behind a tree, in front of the rock).

3. Play "Follow the Leader." Pretend to be going different places and have the children follow (e.g., climbing over rocks, going through tunnels).

Where's the Dinosaur?

by _____

Where's the dinosaur?

Beside the tree.

Where's the dinosaur?

Inside the square. Outside the square.

Where's the dinosaur?

On the chair.

Where's the dinosaur?

Beside the bird.

Where's the dinosaur?

Under the table.

Where's the dinosaur?

Between the bells.

Where's the dinosaur?

On the balloon.

Where's the dinosaur?

Over the balloon.

Where's the dinosaur?

Under the carrot.

Where's the dinosaur?

Over the carrot.

Where's the dinosaur?

In front of the seal.

Where's the dinosaur?

In back of the seal.

Where's the dinosaur?

On the bed.

Where's the dinosaur?

On the big heart.
On the little heart.

Where's the dinosaur?

Going up the stairs.

Where's the dinosaur?

Going down the stairs.

Where's the dinosaur?

_____ •

Where's the dinosaur?

_____ •

 **APPENDIX A**

MONITORING PROGRESS

Name(s): _____   **Date:** _____

_____   **Grade:** _____

Story(ies): _____

_____

Goals: _____

_____

_____

Objectives:	Comment	Comment	Comment
	Date: _____ ___ Mastered ___ Inconsistent ___ Emerging	Date: _____ ___ Mastered ___ Inconsistent ___ Emerging	Date: _____ ___ Mastered ___ Inconsistent ___ Emerging
	Date: _____ ___ Mastered ___ Inconsistent ___ Emerging	Date: _____ ___ Mastered ___ Inconsistent ___ Emerging	Date: _____ ___ Mastered ___ Inconsistent ___ Emerging
	Date: _____ ___ Mastered ___ Inconsistent ___ Emerging	Date: _____ ___ Mastered ___ Inconsistent ___ Emerging	Date: _____ ___ Mastered ___ Inconsistent ___ Emerging
	Date: _____ ___ Mastered ___ Inconsistent ___ Emerging	Date: _____ ___ Mastered ___ Inconsistent ___ Emerging	Date: _____ ___ Mastered ___ Inconsistent ___ Emerging

349

LESSON TRACKING

Pattern Book Title	Snowman, Snowman	Rainbow, Rainbow	Is There a Lion in Your Kitchen?	Is There a Kangaroo in Your Kitchen?	Is There a Gorilla in Your Living Room?	It Looks Like Spilt Milk	Good Morning Sun	Animal Sounds	Whose Toes Are Those?	Somebody's (or [Child's Name]'s) in the Bathtub	What Is Everyone Doing?	Larry Wore His Red Costume	Who Says That?	Where Do You Go to Sleep?	The Important Book	A House Is a House for Me	What Do You Do with a Kangaroo?	City Mouse and Country Mouse	If You Give a Bear an Ice Cream Cone	My Very Own Octopus	Where Does the Brown Bear Go?	A Puppy Is a Puppy
										Dates:												
Group/Child:																						
Group/Child:																						
Group/Child:																						
Group/Child:																						
Group/Child:																						

Pattern Book Title	Guess Where You're Going, Guess What You'll Do	Who Wants One?	I Wish I Could Fly	Who Said Red?	Have You Seen My Toy?	Have You Seen My Pet?	Don't Climb out of the Window Tonight	Sitting in My Tent	Sitting in My Spaceship	These Are My Pets	Hide and Snake	Who Sank the Boat?	Dear Department Store	Dear Restaurant	I Went Walking	This is What I'll Wear	This Is the Bunny	Here Comes a Bus	The Mouse Book	The Elephant Book	How Do You Know?	Where's the Dinosaur?
													Dates:									
Group/Child:																						
Group/Child:																						
Group/Child:																						
Group/Child:																						
Group/Child:																						

LESSON TRACKING—*Continued*

APPENDIX C

PARENT LETTER

Date: _____

Dear Parents,

Your child is bringing home a book that he or she has made in school. The purpose of this book is to continue the learning process at home by reinforcing work done at school. The goal is to have your child tell or read the story while using appropriate communication skills. Your child may not read or say the actual words on the page. This is acceptable and should not be corrected.

Your child is focusing on the following goals:

_____

_____

_____

_____

Listen to your child as he or she shares the book made at school. If you notice your child mispronouncing a word or using a word incorrectly when the story is told, say it correctly for your child so that she or he can hear the correct use. This technique is known as "modeling." Modeling helps your child develop communication skills. Take the opportunity to have your child talk about events that happened in school.

If you have any questions or concerns, please call me at _____.
From time to time, I may send you a parent feedback form, like the one attached, so I can get information about how your child uses his or her communication skills at home. Thank you for your cooperation.

Sincerely,

_____

PARENT FEEDBACK

Date: _____

Dear Parents,

_____ is bringing home a book that he or
(Child's name)
she made. Please have your child read or tell the story to you. After your
child is done reading, respond to the sentences that follow to help me know
about your child's communication at home. Check the blank that best
describes the way your child read her or his book.

1. My child told the story to me
   _____ with my help.   _____ without my help.
   Comments:

2. My child answered questions about the pictures in the book (for example,
   What is that?, What are they doing?, Why would that happen?)
   _____ Yes   _____ No
   Comments:

3. My child pronounced words and sentences correctly.
   _____ Yes   _____ No—If not, please explain:

   _____

4. Another book my child and I read this week was:

   _____

Thank you for completing this feedback form and returning it to me.

Sincerely,

_____

HELPFUL HINTS

HELPFUL HINTS TO ENCOURAGE LITERACY SKILLS AT HOME

1. Read to your child on a regular basis. You may want to have a specific reading time set aside, yet it should not be forced. This time needs to have few distractions. If possible, the reading time should be one on one.

2. Position your child so that he or she can listen to the story and see the story at the same time. Provide a special area where you go to read with your child.

3. Talk about the book you are reading. Take the time to answer questions as your child asks them. Relate the book to experiences you or your child have had.

4. Vary the pace and volume of your voice when you read aloud. Remember to read slowly enough so your child can build a mental picture in his or her mind.

5. Put your finger on the words as you read so your child can follow along. This will help your child to realize that individual words are represented by a group of letters and that a space marks the beginning and end of a word.

6. Read a variety of books, varying the topic and length of the book.

7. Re-read books. Children tend to have favorite books that can be re-read. The repetition is good for remembering, listening, sequencing story parts, and building word knowledge. Each time children hear the story, they understand more about it. This helps them to retell the story.

8. Let your child tell stories to you. Help with new words if he or she needs help.

9. Give your child lots of positive encouragement rather than pointing out errors. He or she will enjoy the experience and want to read more. If your child mispronounces a word or uses a word incorrectly, say it the correct way as a model but let your child continue with the story.

10. Have writing supplies such as paper and pencils available for your child to use. She or he may want to draw pictures of the book you just read or may want to write about it after you read it. (Please note that writing can mean making marks on a paper or writing words and sentences.)

11. Be enthusiastic about books. One way to demonstrate this is to read yourself.

12. Enjoy the time you and your child spend together, and have fun!

REFERENCES

Bankson, N., and Bernthal, J. (1990). *Bankson and Bernthal test of phonology.* Chicago, IL: Riverside.

Creaghead, N. (1992). *Classroom language intervention: Developing schema for school success.* Buffalo, NY: Educom.

Goodman, K. (1986). *What's whole in whole language?* Richmond Hill, Ontario: Scholastic-TAB Publications.

Graden, J., and Bauer, A. (1992). Using a collaborative approach to support students and teachers in inclusive classrooms. In S. Stainback and W. Stainback (Eds.), *Curriculum considerations in inclusive classrooms* (pp. 85–100). Baltimore, MD: Brookes.

Haynes, W., and Shulman, B. (1994). *Communication development: Foundations, processes, and clinical applications.* Englewood Cliffs, NJ: Prentice-Hall.

Johnson, T., and Louis, D. (1990). *Bringing it all together: A program for literacy.* Portsmouth, NH: Heinemann.

Kamhi, A., and Catts, H. (1991). Language and reading: Convergence, divergences, and development. In A. Kamhi and H. Catts (Eds.), *Reading disability: A developmental language perspective* (pp. 1–35, 369–379). Needham Heights, MA: Allyn and Bacon.

Martinez, M., and Roser, N. (1985). Read it again: The value of repeated readings during storytime. *The Reading Teacher, 38,* 782–786.

Marvin, C., and Mirenda, P. (1992, Spring). *Early literacy opportunities for preschool children with disabilities.* Unpublished manuscript, University of Nebraska at Lincoln.

Montgomery, J. (1993, October). *Whole language + speech pathologists + classroom teachers = collaboration!* Unpublished paper presented at the Whole Language Workshop, Milwaukee, WI.

Norris, J., and Damico, J. (1990). Whole language in theory and practice: Implications for language intervention. *Language, Speech, and Hearing Services in Schools, 21*, 212–220.

Norris, J., and Hoffman, P. (1993). *Whole language intervention for school-age children*. San Diego, CA: Singular.

Routman, R. (1991). *Invitations: Changing as teachers and learners K–12*. Portsmouth, NH: Heinemann.

Simon, C. (1991). Introduction—Communication skills and classroom success: Some considerations for assessment and therapy methodologies. In C. Simon (Ed.), *Communication skills and classroom success* (pp. 1–77). Eau Claire, WI: Thinking Publications.

Stanovich, K., Cunningham, A., and Freeman, D. (1984). Intelligence, cognitive skills, and early reading progress. *Reading Research Quarterly, 19*, 279–303.

Sulzy, E. (1989). Forms of writing and rereading from writing. In J. Mason (Ed.), *Reading and writing connections*. Needham Heights, MA: Allyn and Bacon.

van Kleeck, A. (1990). Emergent literacy: Learning about print before learning to read. *Topics in Language Disorders, 10*(2), 25–45.

Wallach, G., and Miller, L. (1988). *Language intervention and academic success*. Austin, TX: Pro-Ed.

Watson, L., Layton, T., Pierce, P., and Abraham, L. (1994). Enhancing emerging literacy in a language preschool. *Language, Speech, and Hearing Services in Schools, 25*, 136–145.

Westby, C. (1991). Learning to talk—Talking to learn: Oral-literate language differences. In C. Simon (Ed.), *Communication skills and classroom success* (pp. 334–357). Eau Claire, WI: Thinking Publications.

Wetherby, A. (1992). *Communication and language intervention for preschool children*. Buffalo, NY: Educom.